NEW REAL-TIME OPERATING SYSTEMS FOR EMBEDDED SYSTEMS

NEW REAL-TIME OPERATING SYSTEMS FOR EMBEDDED SYSTEMS

By

K. SRINIVASA REDDY

M.Tech (Ph.D.)

Associate Prof. Electronics and Communication Engineering

Nagole Institute of Technology and Science

Hyderabad

Andhra Pradesh

UNIVERSITY SCIENCE PRESS

(An Imprint of Laxmi Publications Pvt. Ltd.)

BANGALORE • CHENNAI • COCHIN • GUWAHATI • HYDERABAD
JALANDHAR • KOLKATA • LUCKNOW • MUMBAI • PATNA
RANCHI • NEW DELHI

Published by
UNIVERSITY SCIENCE PRESS
(An Imprint of Laxmi Publications Pvt. Ltd.)
113, Golden House, Daryaganj,
New Delhi-110002
Phone : 011-43 53 25 00
Fax : 011-43 53 25 28
www.laxmipublications.com
info@laxmipublications.com

First Edition : 2013

OFFICES

✆ **Bangalore**	080-26 75 69 30	✆ **Chennai**	044-24 34 47 26
✆ **Cochin**	0484-237 70 04, 405 13 03	✆ **Guwahati**	0361-251 36 69, 251 38 81
✆ **Hyderabad**	040-24 65 23 33	✆ **Jalandhar**	0181-222 12 72
✆ **Kolkata**	033-22 27 43 84	✆ **Lucknow**	0522-220 99 16
✆ **Mumbai**	022-24 91 54 15, 24 92 78 69	✆ **Patna**	0612-230 00 97
✆ **Ranchi**	0651-221 47 64		

UNR–9662–095–NEW REAL-TIME OPER SYS-RED C—

Typeset at ABRO Enterprises, Delhi. *Printed at*
Printed at Repro Knowledgecast Limited, Thane

PREFACE TO THE FIRST EDITION

An embedded operating system (OS) or Real-Time Operating System (RTOS) is a multitasking operating system intended for real-time applications and designed to be very compact and efficient, forsaking many functions that non-embedded computer operating systems provide. An embedded OS or RTOS provides facilities which, if used properly, guarantee deadlines can be met generally (soft real-time) or deterministically (hard real-time). It is valued more for how quickly or predictably it can respond to a particular event than for the amount of work it can perform over a given period of time. Such applications in embedded systems include data processing, automotive industry, healthcare, household appliance controllers, medical monitoring equipment, and consumer electronics.

Every care has been taken to eliminate misprints, omissions and errors but it is too much to expect that no inaccuary/misprint/error has crept in and the author would be grateful to the readers for bringing to his notice any such errors/misprints/omissions they may come across while going through the book.

The author will like to thank the readers (both teachers and students) who sent their valuable suggestions that became the basis for the revision of the book.

The author shall feel satisfied if the book meets the needs of the students for whom it is meant. Suggestions and criticism for improvement of the book are always welcomed.

The author hopes that book will fulfill the need of interested readers and welcome any suggestions towards the improvement of the book.

—Author

ACKNOWLEDGEMENTS

I would like to thank **Prof. Dr N. Satyanarayana, Principal, NITS, Hyderabad** for his valuable supervision and support during the preparation of this book.

I must express my deep appreciation to my wife **Mrs. Geetha Reddy** and my family for their patience, co-operation and understanding which made the tedious task of writing this book much easy to endure.

Special thanks to **N. Uday Kumar** (Research Scholar, ECE, SVU-Tirupathi), **Mr G. Pradeep Reddy** (Assist. Professor, ECE), **Mr M. Ravi Reddy** (Assist. Professor, EEE), **Mr Venkateswar Reddy** (Assist. Professor, EEE) **Mr N. Srinivas Reddy (MS), Mr G. Ram Mohan (MS),** for constant encouragement.

I would like to express my sincere thanks to **Dr K. Lakshma Reddy** chairman of **KLR Group of Institutions. Palvoncha** for constant inspiration and encouragement.

Great care has been taken to produce this book free from errors, but some may remain. I will therefore accept the pleasure any information, which will draw the attention to such mistakes and errors. Criticism about the book shall always be appreciated.

—Author

CONTENTS

Unit 1 INTRODUCTION

- Introduction to UNIX
- Overview of commands
- File I/O (open, create, close, lseek, read, write)
- Process Control (fork, vfork, exit, wait, waitpid, exec)
- Signals
- Interprocess Communication (pipes, fifos, message queues, semaphores, shared memory).

The UNIX 0.5 started on a cast-off DEC PDP-7 at Bell Laboratories in 1969. Ken Thompson with ideas and support from Rudd Canaday, Aoug Melbroy, Jol Ossanna and Dennis Ritchie, wrote a small general purpose time-sharing system comfortable enough to attract enthusiastic users and eventually enough credibility for the purchase of a larger machine—a PDP-11/20. One of the early users was Ritchie, who helped move the system to the PDP-11 in 1970. Ritchie also designed and wrote a compiler for the C programming language in 1973. Ritchie and Thompson rewrote the UNIX kernel in C, breaking from the tradition that systen software is written in assembly language.

What makes the UNIX sys. so successful? We consider several reasons. First, because it is written in C, it is portable—UNIX sys. run on a range of computers from UPS to the largest main-frames this is a strong commercial advantage.

Second, the source code is available and written in a Hi-level language which makes the sys. easy to adapt to particular requirements. Finally, most important it is a good operating system, specially for programmers. The UNIX programming environment is usually rich and productive.

WHAT IS "UNIX"?

In the narrowest sense, it is a time-sharing O.S. kernel a program that controls the resources of a computer and allocates them among its users. It lets users run their programs; it controls the peripheral devices (discs, terminals, pointer connected to the machine and it provides a file system, that manages the long-term storage of information such as programs, data and documents. In a broader sense, "UNIX" is often taken to include not only the kernel, but also essential programs like compilers, editors command languages, programs for copying and printing files, and so on.

UNIX is an operating system which was first developed in the 1960s, and has been under constant development over since. By operating system, we mean the suite of programs which make the computer work. It is a stable, multi-user, multi-tasking system for servers, desktops and laptops.

UNIX systems also have a graphical user interface (GUI) similar to Microsoft Windows which provides an easy to use environment. However, knowledge of UNIX is required for operations which aren't covered by a graphical program, or for when there is no windows interface available, for example, in a telnet session.

TYPES OF UNIX

There are many different versions of UNIX, although they share common similarities. The most popular varieties of UNIX are Sun Solaris, GNU/ Linux, and MacOS X.

Here in the School, we use Solaris on our servers and workstations, and Fedora Linux on the servers and desktop PCs.

THE UNIX OPERATING SYSTEM

The UNIX operating system is made up of **three** parts;

- Kernel
- Shell
- Programs.

The Kernel

The kernel of UNIX is the hub of the operating system: it allocates time and memory to programs and handles the file store and communications in response to system calls.

The Shell

The shell acts as an interface between the user and the kernel. When a user logs in, the login program checks the username and password and then starts another program called the shell. The shell is a command line interpreter (CLI). It interprets the commands the user types in and arranges for them to be carried out. The commands are themselves programs: when they terminate, the shell gives the user another prompt (% on our systems).

FILES AND PROCESSES

Everything in UNIX is either a file or a process.

A process is an executing program identified by a unique PID (process identifier).

A file is a collection of data. They are created by users using text editors, running compilers etc.

Examples of files:

- a document (report, essay etc.);
- the text of a program written in some high-level programming languages;
- instructions comprehensible directly to the machine and incomprehensible to a casual user, for example, a collection of binary digits (an executable or binary file);
- a directory, containing information about its contents, which may be a mixture of other directories (sub-directories) and ordinary files.

THE DIRECTORY STRUCTURE

All the files are grouped together in the directory structure. The file-system is arranged in a hierarchical structure, like an inverted tree. The top of the hierarchy is traditionally called **root** (written as a slash /)

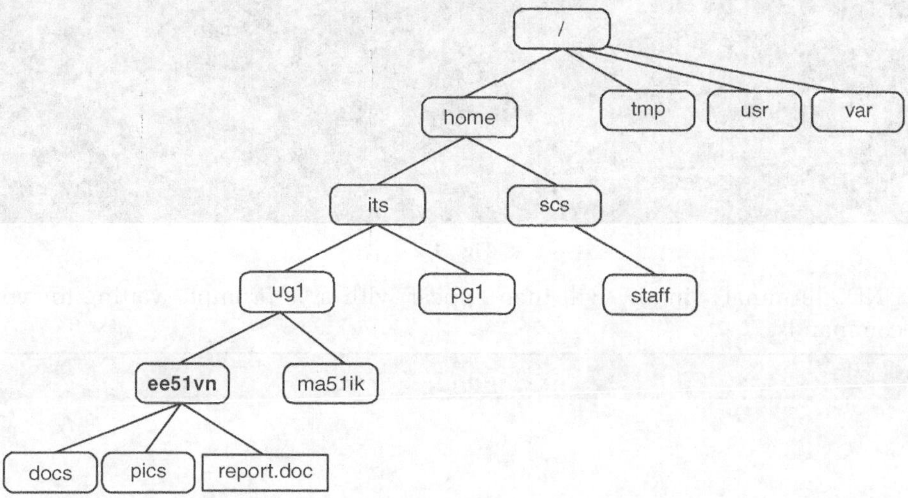

Fig. 1.1

In the diagram above, we see that the home directory of the undergraduate students **"ee51vn"** contains two sub-directories (**docs** and **pics**) and a file called **report.doc.**

The full path to the file **report.doc** is **"/home/its/ug1/ee51vn/report.doc".**

STARTING AN UNIX TERMINAL

To open an UNIX terminal window, click on the "Terminal" icon from the drop-down menus.

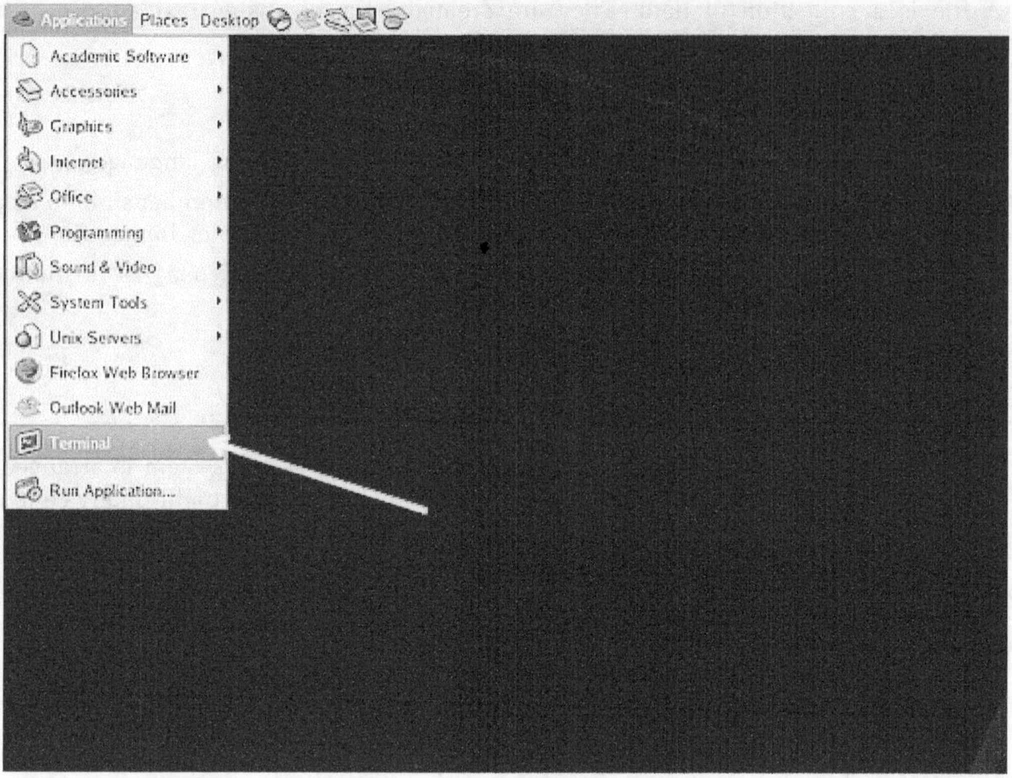

Fig. 1.2

An UNIX Terminal window will then appear with a % prompt, waiting for you to start entering commands.

Fig. 1.3

OVERVIEW OF COMMANDS IN UNIX

- **tail**

  These commands used to print last 10 lines in a file.

  syntax: $ *tail* file name

  $ *tail*-1 file name print only last line of file

  $ *tail*-n file name print last n lines of file

  $ *tail*+n file name start printing file at line n

- **compare**

  These are used to print location of first difference.

  syntax: $ cmp file1 file2

- **difference**

  These are used to print all differences b/w files.

  syntax: $ diff file1 file2

- **pwd (print working directory)**

  $ pwd /usr/you

  This is says that you are currently in which directory, in directory user, which in turn is in the root directory. Which is conventionally called just '/'. The / characters separate the components of the name: The limit of 14 characters mentioned above applies to each component of such a name.

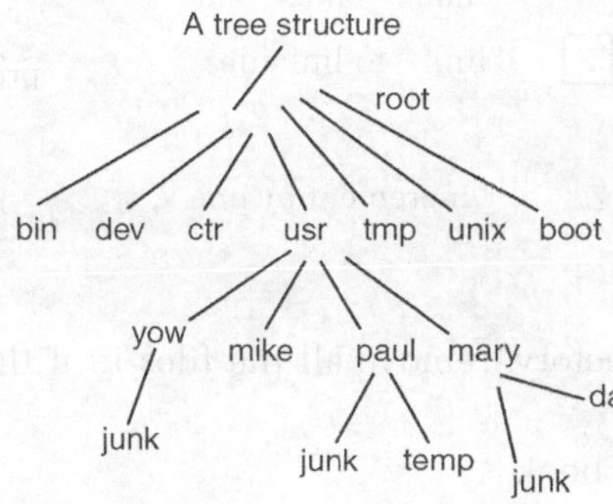

Fig. 1.4

→ Cat is used to display the content of file on the screen.

syntax: $ cat / usr / you / junk

- **ls**

  list names of all files in current directory.

  syntax: $ls ↵

$ls file names ↵	list only the named files
$ls-t	list in time order, most recent first
$ls-l	list long: more information; $lsuslt

$ls-u	list by time last used; $lsuslu, $lsuslut
$ls-r	list in reverse order; $ -rt, -rlt

- **edit**

  syntax: $ed file name edit named file

  Ex.: $ed /usr/mary/data

- **copy**

  syntax: $cp file1 file2 copy file1 to file2, overwrite file2 if it exists

  Ex.: $cp /usr/mary/data data

  make your own copy of one of her files

- **move**

  syntax: $ mv file1 file2 move file1 to file2

- **changing directory**

  This is used to changing your current directory.

  syntax: $cd /usr/mary

- **make a directory (create a directory)**

  This is used to make a new directory

  syntax: $mkdir book $mkdir path x y

  $mkdir pis/prog pis/data

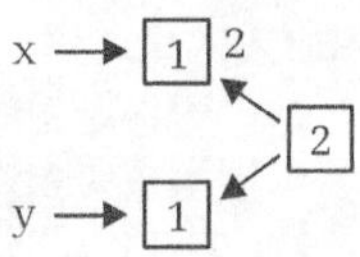

inode – index node

link – to link files

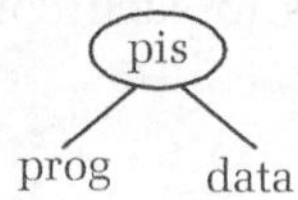

$ ln × Z increment by one x, y

- **remove directory**

  To remove the directory, remove all the files in it then cd to the parent directory or book and type

  syntax: $ rmdir book

  $ rmdir pis rmdir will only remove an empty directory

- **link**

  Used to link b/w files.

  syntax: $ ln cmp.ls_t cmp

  $ ln cmp.ls_t cmp.data

- **unlink (remove link)**

  syntax: $ unlink X decrement by 1

  $unlink Y

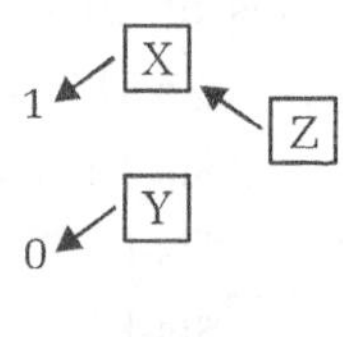

- **absolute pathnames**

Unix command have first file name, director argument in current directories.

$cat login.file $cat /home/ksr/login.sql

Two types of path names

→ relative pathname: without '/'

→ Absolute pathname: start with '/' the

Ex.: $cd /paul/junk

$cat /usr/mary/data

Ex.: $cd programs

$cd scripts $cd programs/scripts

- **common**

This is used to give the common's in two files required to shorted files.

syntax: $comm

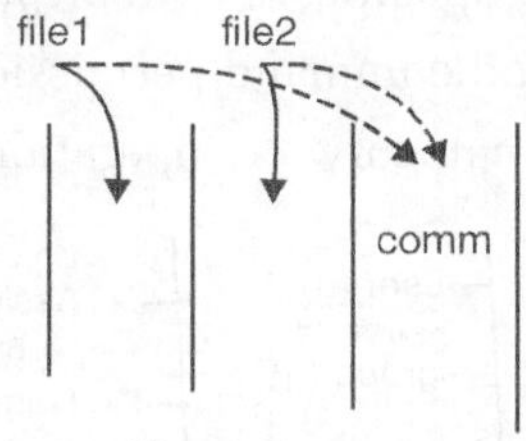

Fig. 1.5

- **od (octal dump)**

Which is used to display the non-visible character like **tap**. Newline char **back space**

$od-b file1 → to display ASCII values of char's in a file.

$od-bc file1 → including char's/root

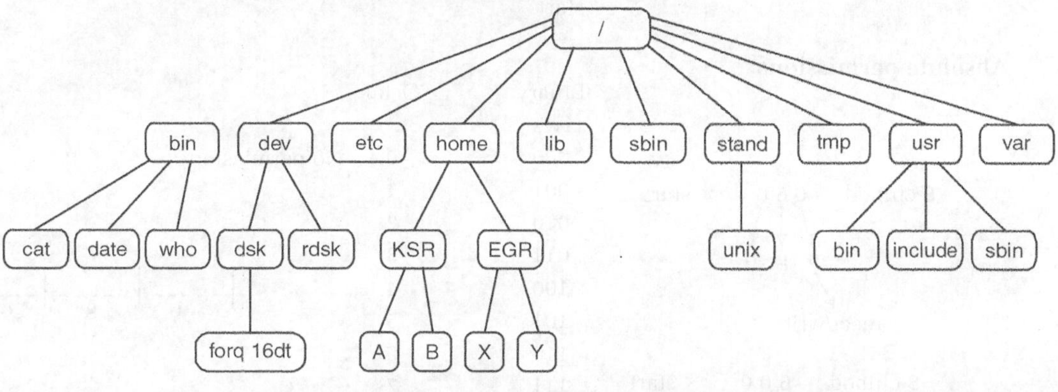

Fig. 1.6

→ some commands are executed by administrator only for such commands, used to configure the system.

- **head**

  display the top of the file without options with first 10 lines of a file to the screen.

  syntax: $head – n tmp.txt before using this command first "clear the screen".

- **changing mode:** (*a*) changing file permissions.

  These are sends only by user one or more users, others **chmod** is a command to change the file permissions.

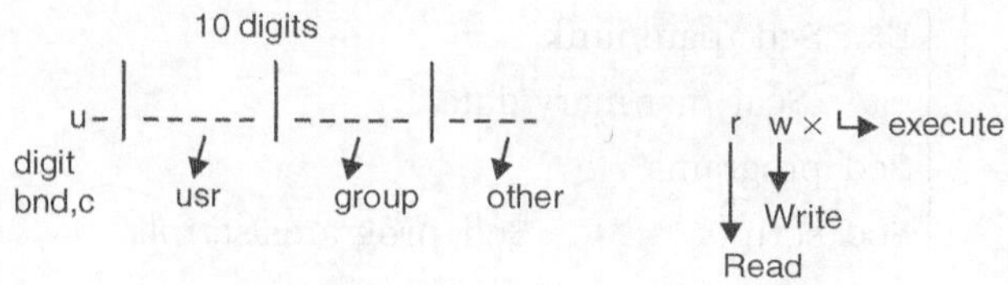

Used two ways

→ Relative manner: current positions make changes

→ Absolute manner: specifies the final permission.

relative permissions: chmod command permissions leave other permissions unchanged.

syntax: $ chmod category operation permission filenames.

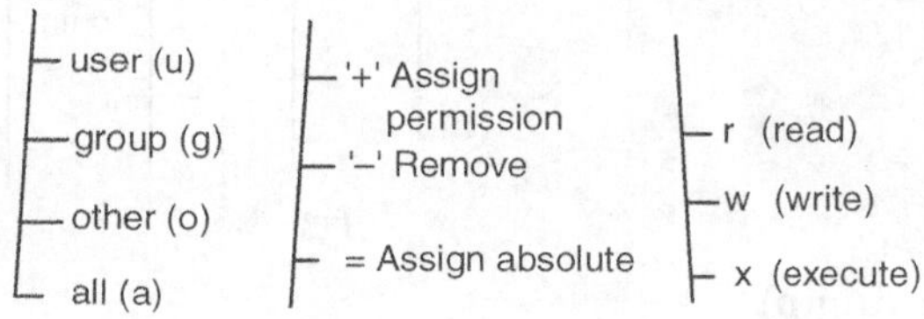

To change the permission of a file current user must be a owner of the file or sys. admin.

$ chmode u + x file name

↓

start

Absolute permissions:

Binary	Octal	
rwx		
000	0	No permissions
001	1	
010	2	
011	3	
100	4	
101	5	
110	6	
111	7	

$ chmod 6 6 6 × start

↓ ↓ ↓

u g o

↙

react/write

$ chmod 6 0 0 × start

↓ ↓ ↓

u – –

↙

R/w

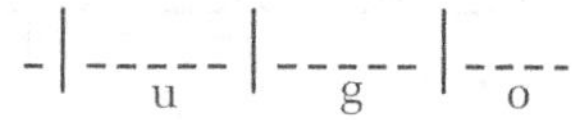

- **changing file ownership:** It requires super user permission.

  1st change our status to the super user with **su** command.

  syntax: $su ↵ ask password sys. administator ↵ xxxxxx

  $chown ksr note #chown[new owner name] [file name]

  $ls-l – ≠ ×××|×××|×××|link/or/metal/data.time note

- **changing groupowner:** This is used to change groupowner

  syntax: $chgrp dba note

- **calendar:** see calendar of specific month or year

  syntax: call [[month] year]

  $cal current month

  $cal 07 2007

- **date**

  Used to display current date

  $date ↵

  Mon Mar 05 ......

  also be used with suitable format specified as arguments format specified by '+' symbol forward by % operation single char displayed.

  $date +% m ↵ current month no. displayed

  $date +% h ↵ name of the current month displayed

  $date +% d ↵ day of the month specified

  y ↵ last two digits of year displayed

  D ↵ date format mm/dd/yy

  T ↵ hh: mm: ss

  y ↵ four digits of year

- **echo**

  Used to display a message or to evaluate shell variables

  $echo "Hello" ↵ double quote is optional

  $echo Hello

  The shell is just an ordinary program like date or who the fact that the shell site between you and the facilities of the kernel has real benefits.

- **who**

  These give the details of user's who logged onto the unix sys.

  $who usr2 tty1

- **tty (three type command)**

  Display terminal currently u'r using it.

  $tty ↵

  Ex: dev/pts/10 then display the current terminal you are using.

- **finger**

  More informations abt users of particular host machine.

  $finger

  fingure@host name

- **tput clear screen**

  $tput clear ↵

- **calculator**

  syntax: $bc ↵ $ bc

  CURSOR blinking

  ctrl-d quit the calculator

- **find**

  Used for locating files, which directory files are there

  $Find path-list selection criteria action

  $find/–namea.out - print

  Locating files by inod no.

  $find path-list inode no. action

  $find /–inum 13975 – print

- **cut**

  Used for slitting file vertically and extracting

  a columns & fields of files.

  –c –f

  - **Cutting columns:** To extract specific columns one as to allow the **c** options deliminate by symbol "," (comma)

    $cut –c 6 –22, 24–32, short list

  - **Cutting fields:**

    length of lines are fixed use '–c'

    length of lines are varies '–f'

    –d field deliminiter |, |

    –f field existing field separated by |, |

    $ cut –d "1"

    $ cut –d \ |–f 2, 3 short list

    $ cut –d "1"|–f 1, 4, 5, 6 short list

- **Paste**

  Used to paste two files side by side

  $ paste cut list1 cut list2

- **The shell**

  Shell is a program b/w user & kernel

  $cut G.list

  ↓

  shell

- **wc**

  Counting lines, words, chars

  $wc files1

3 20 50 file1
urg words char.

$wc - l file1 → to display only lines
$wc - w file1 → to display only words
$wc - c file1 → to display only char
$wc - lw → to display lines and words
$wc - lc → to display lines and char
$wc - wc → to display words and char

- **sleep**

  to take the shell into sleeping state

  $ sleep [time in sec]

  $ sleep 5

- **executing multiple commands**

  $cmd1; cmd2; cmd3

  Ex.: $lc; sleep5; date

- **create a file**

  $cat >[filename]

  Ex.: $cat >file1

  This is K.S. Reddy student of AITS.

- **Displaying file contents**

  $cat < [filename]
  ↓
  optional

  Ex.: $cat < file1

  This is EGR

- **Displaying multiple files**

  $cat file1 file2 file3

- wild card characters (also called **meta char**)

  * → any no. of chars

  ? → only one char.

  These char are used to naming the files.

  $ls* to → display all files

  $cp./* /home/user2/y → to copy the all files from current working directory to 'y' directory.

  $ls *.* → files with extension only

  $ls *. cpp → only c++ files

  $ls *.? → to display files with only one char as extension

  $ls *.?? → to display files with only two char as extension

$ls f* → to display files start with char 'f'

$ls f??? → to display files with at least four chars and start with f

$ls file[1–9] → to display file1 to file9

$ls file[!1–9] → to display file start with "file" and not followed with 1–9

- **unmask**

  Default file and directory permission

  regular file → 666

  directory file → 777

$ umask 222	666 222 444	777 222 555
$ umask 111	666 111 555	

$ umask 000 →to change the mask value

umask value tells that not to grant specified permissions.

- **working with shell**

  Unix provides **three** types of shells

  → bourne shell

  → k-shell

  → c-shell

  Default shell is bourne shell and it's as mostly used shell.

  Working with bourne shell it provides the commands, keywords, control statements and operators to develop the shell scripting.

- **user limit**

  The max. size of file, user to permit create a file.

  # ulimit 600

- **Command substitution into the text:**

  command quotations " 'cmd' " are used to substitute them into the text.

  quotations key → Below the "ESC" key

Quoting: When common argument enclosed in quotes the meaning of the all enclosed special char's are turn off.

$rm 'chap*' single quotes projects all special chars excepts itself.

$rm chap/* "double quotes don't project itself the dollar backquotes $ ≠.

Filters

Pipe, head, tail, tr, tee and grep and fgrep

- **pipe**

  This is for inter process communication

$ cmd1 ≠ cmd2

cmd1............pipe.........**cmd2**

cmd1 o/p will be write to the pipe and it will be taken by cmd2

Ex.: $ls - 1/pg

$cat < file1|wc-l

30 → no. of lines in a file1

$who|wc-l

u → no. of present working users

- **Translation command (tr)**

To replace the character.

$tr "oldchar" "new char" <[filename]

$tr "a" "z" <file1

tr command replace the "oldchar" with "newchar".

$tr "a" "z" <file1 > filex

To redirect the replaced out to **filex** silently redirect the o/p to the filex.

$cat filex

- **tee command**

it works with pipe

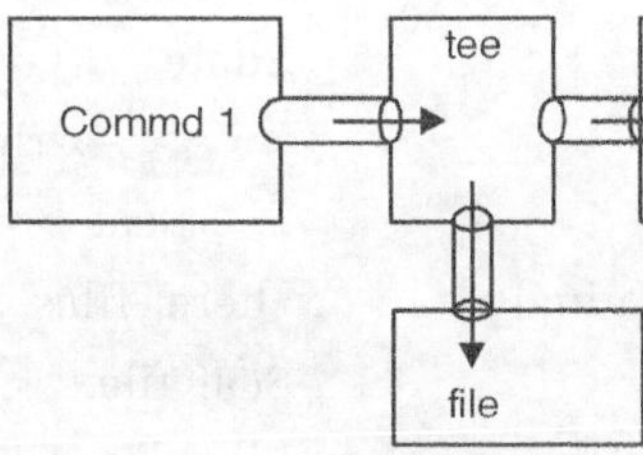

Fig. 1.7

$command1|command2|

$command1|tee file| command2 storage on to disk

$cat <file1|tee filex

it display the o/p on the screen as well as send to the filex.

$date|tee filex

- **Grep command**

Used to pattern searching

$grep "searching pattern" [file name]

grep command displays the lines in which searching pattern is found.

$grep "hello" [file name]

$grep -n "searching pattern" [file name] → including line no.,

$grep -v "searching pattern" [file name]

displays the lines in which searching pattern is not found.

- **Standard files of unix**

  They are 3 standard files of unix

  → std i/p file – Standard input file

  → std o/p file – Standard output file

  → std error file – Standard error file

  std i/p file → The file or stream represents i/p, which is connected to keyboard.

  std o/p file → The file stream represents o/p, which is connected to display.

  std error file → The file stream represents error message, which is connected to display.

- **Standard i/p: Standard input file**

  Keyboard, the default source.

  $wc

  KSR technologies

  Ameerpet Hyd

  ^d 3 4 48

  A file using redirection with the <symbol

  < → is a left side redirection

  $wc < sample. txt

  $cat < file1

- **Standard o/p file**

  Default std output file terminal (destination)

  $cat file1

  KSR technologies

  Ameerpet, hyd.

  Here, default o/p is terminal

  $date > filex

  $date

  > → right side redirection

  $cat > file1

  here, files is o/p file.

  $cat filex

  $ls - l > filex

  if filex is already exist then it overwrite

  >> → to append to the file.

- **std error file**

  $cat filey

  cat: can't open file y

  cat open the file writes to standard error

  $cat filey > filex

  $cat filex → no output

  using > can't send to the filex.

  0 → std. i/p

  1 → std. o/p

  2 → std. error

  To redirect error messages to file

  $cat filey 2 > filex

  $cat filex

Back-up Programs

Back-up commands: **cpio/tar** two back-up programs

- **cpio (Copy input output)** **Ex.:** Flopy ≈ 1.44 MB

  archive: A group of files or entire directory.

  cpio combined a group of files into archive.

  c → create new archival file

  v → VERBOSE is security protocol

  f → specified files.

  Back up files

  ```
  $ ls |cpio -ov >/dev/rdsk/foq/18dt
  ```

  an archive verbose: display each file while copy

  ```
  $cpio – ov > /dev/rdsk/foq18dt < filename
  ```

- **Incremental backup**

  block size 5120 bytes

  ```
  $ls*.pl/cpio- ovb > / dev / rdsk / foq 18 dt
  $ls*.pl/cpio - ovc 51200 > /dev / rdsk / foq 18 dt
  ```

  ↓

  set the block size to be 5120 a > 5210

  Two backup programs—cpio and tar. Both combine a group of files into an archive. The backup device can be a magnetic or a cartridge tape, a floppy diskette or even a disk file.

CPIO

The cpio command (copy i/p o/p) copies files to and from a backup device. It uses standard i/p to take the list of file names. It then copies them with their contents and headers to a stream which can be redirected to a file or a device. This means that cpio can be used with redirection and piping.

cpio uses two key options

–o (o/p)

–i (i/p) either of which must be there in the command line.

The –v (verbose) option displays each filename on the terminal when its being copied. cpio needs as i/p a list of files and if this list is available in a file redirection can be used too:

```
cpio –o >/dev/rdsk/foq18dt < flist.
```

Restoring Files (–i)

A complete archive or selected files can be restored with the –i key option. To restore files use redirection to take i/p from the device.

```
# cpio –iv < /dev/rdsk/foq18dt
```

cpio also accepts a quoted wild-card pattern, so multiple files fitting the pattern can be restored. Restoring only the shell scripts becomes quite easy.

cpio –i "*.sh" < /dev/rdsk/foq18dt

Handling modification times (–m) By default, when a file is extracted its modification time is set to the time of extraction.

Displaying the Archive (–it)

The –t option displays the contents of the device without restoring the files. This option must be combined with the –i key option:

cpio –itv < /dev/rdsk/foq18dt

Other Options

There are two important options that can be used with the –o and –i options:

- The –r (rename) option lets you rename each file before starting the copying process. The sys. presents each filename and prompts you for a response.
- The –f option followed by an expression causes cpio to select all files except those in the expression.

  cpio –ivf "*.c" </dev/rdsk/foq18dt

tar: The "TAPE" Archive program

The tar command has been in existence since before the emergence of cpio. It is a versatile command with certain exclusive features not found in cpio:

- It doesn't standard i/p to obtain its file list. tar accepts file and directory names as arguments.
- It copies one or more entire directory tress *i.e.,* it operates recursively by default.
- It can append to an archive without overwriting the entire archive.

Backup Files (–c)

tar accepts directory and filenames directly on the command line. The –c key option is used to copy files to the backup file. The verbose option (–v) shows the progress of the backup.

tar –cvf /dev/rdsk/foq18dt/home/sales/SQL/*. sql

The a before each pathname indicates that the file is appended. The command backup all SQL scripts with their absolute pathnames.

key option	singnificance
–c	create a new archive
–x	extracts files from archive
–t	lists contents of archive
–r	Appends files at end of archive
–u	like r, but only if files are newer than those in archive.

Restoring Files (–x)

Files are restored with the –x (extract) key option. When no file or directory name is specified, it restores all files from the backup device.

tar –xvfb /dev/rdsk/foq18dt 18

Selective extraction is also possible by providing one or more directory or filenames

tar –xvf /dev/rdsk/foq18dt/home/sales/SQL/t_mr_allocs

Displaying the Archive (–t)

Like in cpio the –t key option displays the contents of the device in a long format 11y to the listing.

tar –tvf /dev/rdsk/foq18dt

SUMMARY OF UNIX COMMANDS

Command	Meaning
Ls	list files and directories
ls –a	list all files and directories
Mkdir	Make a directory
cd *directory*	change to named directory
Cd	change to home-directory
cd ~	change to home-directory
cd ..	change to parent directory
Pwd	display the path of the current directory
cp file1 file2	copy file1 and call it file2
mv file1 file2	Move or rename file1 to file2
rm file	remove a file
Rmdir directory	remove a directory
cat file	display a file
less file	display a file a page at a time
head file	display the first few lines of a file
tail file	display the last few lines of a file
grep 'keyword' file	search a file for keywords
wc file	Count number of lines/words/characters in file

Command	Meaning
command > file	redirect standard output to a file
command >> file	append standard output to a file
command < file	redirect standard input from a file
command1 | command2	pipe the output of command1 to the input of command2
cat file1 file2 > file0	concatenate file1 and file2 to file0
Sort	sort data
Who	list users currently logged in
*	Match any number of characters
?	Match one character
What is command	brief description of a command
ls -lag	list access rights for all files
Chmod [*options*] *file*	change access rights for named file
command &	run command in background
^C	kill the job running in the foreground
^Z	suspend the job running in the foreground
Bg	background the suspended job
Jobs	list current jobs
fg %1	foreground job number 1
kill %1	kill job number 1
Ps	list current processes

FILE I/O

File Descriptors

To the kernel all open files are referred to by file descriptors. A file descriptor is a non- negative integer. When we open an existing file or create a new file, the kernel returning a file descriptive to the process. When we want to read or write a file, we identify the file with the file discriptor that was returned by **open** or **create** as an argument to either **read** or **write.**

File descriptors range from O through OPEN - MAX. Older version of unix had an upper limit of 19 (allowing a max. of 20 open files per process) but this was increased to 63 by many systems.

Topic: File Descriptors

Most UNIX file I/O boils down to five functions:

- open
- read
- write
- lseek
- close

Important Points of File Descriptor

- Kernel refers to open files by file descriptors.
- File descriptor is non-negative integer.
- Convention: 0 is stdin, 1 is stdout, 2 is stderr.
- POSIX defines STDIN FILENO, STDOUT FILENO, STDERR FILENO in <unistd.h>
- Each process has a fixed size descriptor table, which is guaranteed to

Have at least n slots.

- The entries in the descriptor table are numbered with small integers

Starting at 0.

- The call getdtablesize(3) returns the size of this table.

Open Function

A file is created or opened by calling the open fun.

int open (const) char *pathname, int of log, .../*, mode-t mode*/);

0 – on success

–1– an error returns by **f.d**

- 3rd argument as......., which is the ANSI c way to specify that the number and symbol remaining arguments may vary.
- The 3rd argument is only used when a new file is being created.
- The pathname is the name of the file to open or create. There are a multitude of options for this function, which are specified by the **oflog** argument. This argument is formed by **ORing** together one or more of the following constants.

O – RDONLY open for reading only

O – WRONLY open for writing only

O – RDWR open for RD & WR

One and only one of these three constants must be specified.

The following constants are optional:

O – APPEND	Append to the end of file on each write
O – CREAT	Creat the file if it doesn't exist
O – EXCL	Generate an error if file is already exist
O – TRUNC	if the file exists and successfully opened to either WR only or RD – WR truncate its length to O.
O – NOCTTY	if the pathname refers to a terminal device
O – NONBLOCK	if the pathname refers to a FIFO a block special file or a character special file
O – SYNC	Have each write wait for physical i/o to complete.

Important Points of Open Function

- flags are formed by OR'ing.
- success: returns a non-negative integer (file descriptor).
- open guarantees to return the lowest numbered unused descriptor.
- failure: –1 and errno is set to indicate the error.
- *E.g.*, ENAMETOOLONG: A component of a pathname exceeded NAME MAX.
- creat(3) is the same as:
- open(path, O CREAT | O TRUNC | O WRONLY, mode);

Creat Function

A new file as can be created by these file descriptors

int creat (const char. *pathname, mode-t mode)

0+onsuccess

–1–an error

Note that this fun is equivalent to

open (pathname, O_WRONLY |O_CREAT |O_TRUNC, mode) ;

One deficiency with creat is that the file is opened only for writing. A better way is to use the new open fun as in

open (pathname, O_RDWR|O_CREAT|O_TRUNC, mode);

Close Function

An open file is closed by

int close (int files);

0 – on success

– 1 – an error

closing a file also releases any record locks that the process may have on the file. When a process terminates all open files are automatically closed by the kernel.

Important Points of Close Function

- When a process exits, all associated file descriptors are freed.

- close(2) may be used to not run out of active descriptors per process.
- returns 0 on success, -1 on failure and sets global int errno.
- close(2) will fail if:
- Argument is not an active descriptor (EBADF).
- An interrupt was received (EINTR).

lseek Function

Every open file has an associated "current file offset". This is a non-negative integer that measures the no. of bytes from the beginning of the file. By default, this offset is initialized to O when a file is opened, unless the O – APPEND option is specified.

An open file can be explicitly positioned by calling **lseek**

off_t lseek (int filedes, off _t offset, int whence);

0 – on success

–1 – an error

The interpretation of the offset depends on the value of the **whence** argument:

- if whence is SEEK_SET, the file's offset is set to offset bytes from the beginning of the file.
- if whence is SEEK_CUR, the file's offset is set to its current value plug the offset. The offset can be +ve or –ve.
- if whence is SEEK_END, the file's offset is set to the size of file plug the offset. The offset can be +ve or –ve.

Since a successful call to a **lseek** returns the new file offset we can seek zero bytes from the current position determine the current offset.

off_t currpos;

⇓

lseek (fd, o, SEEK_CUR);

This technique can also be used to determine if the referenced file is capable of **seeking.**

Read Function

Data is read from an open file with the read fun.

ssize_t read (int filedes, void *buff, size_t n bytes);

no. of bytes read, 0 if end of file

–1 on error.

- If the read is successful, the number of bytes read is returned, if the end of file is encountered, o is returned.
- There are several cases in which the number of bytes actually read is less than the amount requested:
  - when reading from a regular file, if the end of file is reached before the requested number of bytes has been read.
  - when reading from a terminal device, normally up to one line is read at a time
  - when reading from a N/W, buffering within the N/W may cause less than the requested amount to be returned.

- some record – oriented devices, such as a magnetic tape, return upto a single record at a time.

The read operation starts at the file's current offset. Before a successful return, then offset is incremented by the number of bytes actually read.

Int read (int filedes, char* butt, unsigned n bytes);

Standard the new primitive data type ssize_t was introduced to provide the signed return value, and the unsigned size_t was used for the 3rd argument.

Important Points of Read Function

- read nbytes to buffer buf.
- returns number of bytes read, 0 if EOF, –1 on failure.
- number of bytes returned is often smaller than requested.
- read starts at current offset and increments current offset.

Write Function

Data is written to an open file with the write function.

ssize_t write (int filedes, const void *buff, size_t n bytes);

0 – no. of bytes written

–1 – an error

The return value is usually equal to the n bytes argument, otherwise an error has occurred. A common cause for a write error is either filling up a disk or exceeding the file size limit for a given process. After a successful write. The files offset is ↑ by the number of bytes actually written.

Important Points of Write Function

- nbytes of data in buf are written to open file d.
- Return value is usual equal to nbytes, otherwise an error occurred.
- Other errors are indicated by –1 and errno.
- Write increments file's offset.

PROCESS CONTROL

Process Identifiers

Every process has a unique process ID, a non–ve integer. Since the process ID is the only well-known identifier of a process *i.e.*, always unique, it is often used as a piece of other identifiers to guarantee uniqueness.

- The **tmpnam** fun created unique pathnames by incorporating the process ID in the name. There are some special processes.
- Process ID 0 is usually the scheduler process and is often known as the **swapper** no program on disk corresponds to this process it is part of the kernel is known as a system process.
- Process ID 1 is usually the **init** process and is invoked by the kernel at the end of the bootstrap procedure. The program file for this process was /etc/init and /sbin/init. The **init** process never dies.

- One some virtual memory implementations of unix, process ID 2 is the **pagedaemon**. This process is responsible for supporting the paging of the virtual mem. system. swapper and pagedaemon is a kernel process. In addition to the process ID, there are other identifiers for every process.

pid _t getpid (void)	process ID of calling process
pid _t getpaid (void)	parent process of calling process
uid _t getuid (viod)	real user ID of calling process
uid _t geteuid (viod)	effective user ID of calling process
gid _t getgid (viod)	real group ID of calling process
gid _t getegid (viod)	effective group ID of calling process

Note that none of these fun's has an error return.

fork Function

The only way a new process is created by the unix kernel is when an existing process calls the **fork** function. The swaper, init and the pagedaemon. These processes are created specially by the kernal as part of the boots stropping.

pid _t fork (void);

0 – inchild, process ID of child in parent

–1– on an error.

- The new process created by fork is called the "child process". This fork function is called once but returns twice. The only difference in the returns is that the return value in the child is 'O' while the return value in the parent is the process ID of the new child. The reason the child's process ID is returned to the parent is because a process can have more than one child, so there is no function that allows a process to obtain the process IDs of its children.
- The reason **fork** returns O to the child is because a process can have only a single parent, so the child can always call **getppid** to obtain the process ID of its parent.
- Both the child and parent continue executing with the instruction that follows the call to **fork**. The child is a copy of the parent.
- Many current implementations don't perform a complete copy of the parent's data stack & heap since a fork is often followed by an exec. Instead, a technique called "copy-on-write (cow)" is used.
- These regions are shared by the parent and child and have their protections changed by the kernel to read-only.

```
int main(void)
{
    pid_t pid;
    printf ("Before fork \n");
        pid = fork();
    if (pid >0)
    {
        sleep (1)
        printf ("PARENT...PID: %d ppid, %d CHILD PID, %din", get pid(), get pidprid);
    }
```

```
else
    if (pid= =0)
printf ("CHILD...PID: %d ppid, %d in", get pid(), get ppid ());
else
{
    print f("fork error"\n);
        exit (1);
}
printf("Both process continues from fork \n");
exit (0);
}
```

File Sharing between Parent Process Table–Child Process Table

When we redirect the standard o/p of the parent, the child standard o/p is also redirected. One characteristic of **fork** is that all descriptors that are open in the parent are duplicated in the child.

Consider a process that has three different files opened for standard i/p, o/p and error,

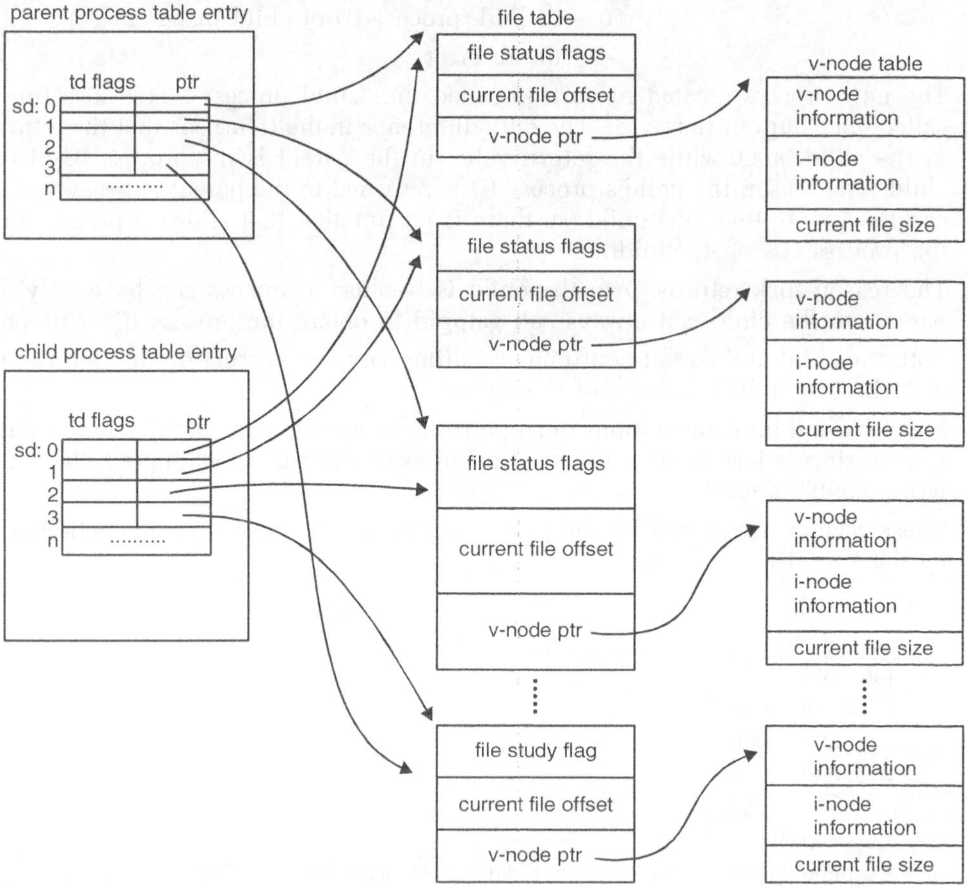

Fig. 1.8

Sharing of open files b/w parent and child after **fork** if both parent and child write to the same descriptor, without any form of synchronization, then o/p will be intermixed (assuming its a descriptor that was open before the fork). While this is possible, its not the normal mode of operation. There arc two normal cases for handling the descriptors after a fork:

- The parent waits for the child to complete.
- The parent and child each go their own way. Here, after the fork, the parent close the descriptors that it doesn't need and the child dose the same thing.

Besides the open files, there are numerous other properties of the parent that are inherited by the child.

- real user ID, real group ID, effective user ID, effective group ID
- supplementary group IDS
- process group IDS
- session ID
- controlling terminal
- environments
- resources limits
- set-user-ID flag and set-group-ID flag
- current working directory
- root directory
- file mode creation mask
- signal mask, dispositions
- attached shared mem segments

The differences between the parent and child was:

- the return value from fork
- the processes IDS are different
- the two processes have different parent processes IDS - the parent process ID of the child is the parent: The parent process ID of the parent doesn't change.
- the child's values for tms-utime, tms-stime, tms_cutime and tms_ustime are set to O.
- file locks set by the parent are not inherited by the child.
- pending alarms are cleared for the child.
- the set of pending signals for the child is set to the empty set.

The two main reasons for fork to fail are:

- if there are already too many processes in the system.
- if the total number of processes for this real user ID exceeds the system's limit.

vfork Function

The function vfork has the same calling sequence and same return values as fork. But the semantics of the two functions suffer.

Vfork is intended to create a new process when the purpose of the new processing to **exec** a new program. Vfork creates the new process, just like fork, without fully copying the address space of the parent into the child. Since, the child won't reference that address space the child just calls **exec** (exit) right after the vfork. Instead, while the child is running, until it calls either **exec** or exit, the child runs in the address space of the parent.

Another difference b/w the two functions is that **vfork** guarantees that the child runs first. Until the child calls exec or exit. When the child calls either of these functions, the parent resumes.

What's the Difference between fork( ) and vfork( )?

The system call vfork( ), is a low overhead version of fork( ), as fork( ) involves copying the entire address space of the process and is therefore quite expensive.

The basic difference between the two is that when a new process is created with vfork( ), the parent process is temporarily suspended, and the child process might borrow the parent's address space. This strange state of affairs continues until the child process either exits, or calls execve( ), at which point the parent process continues. This means that the child process of a vfork( ) must be careful to avoid unexpectedly modifying variables of the parent process. In particular, the child process must not return from the function containing the vfork( ) call, and it must not call exit( ) (if it needs to exit, it should use _exit( ); actually, this is also true for the child of a normal fork( )). However, since vfork( ) was created, the implementation of fork( ) has improved, most notably with the introduction of 'copy-on-write', where the copying of the process address space is transparently faked by allowing both processes to refer to the same physical memory until either of them modify it. This largely removes the justification for vfork( ); indeed, a large proportion of systems now lack the original functionality of vfork( ) completely. For compatibility, though, there may still be a vfork( ) call present, that simply calls fork( ) without attempting to emulate all of the vfork( ) semantics.

What's a Zombie Process?

When using fork( ) to create child processes it is important to keep track of these processes. For instance, when a child process terminates, an association with the parent survives untill the parent either terminates normally or calls wait( ). The child process entry in the process table is not freed up immediately. Although, it is no longer active, the child process is still in the system because it's exit code needs to be stored in the even the parent process calls wait(). **The child process is at that point referred to as a zombie process**. Note, if the parent terminates abnormally then the child process gets the process with PID 1, (init) as parent. (**Such a child process is often referred to as an orphan**). The child process is now a zombie. It is no longer running, it's original parent process is gone, and it has been inherited by init. It will remain in the process table as a zombie until the next time the table is processed. If the process table is long this may take a while till init cleans them up. As a general rule, program wisely and try to avoid zombie processes.

When zobbies accumulate they eat up valuable resources. The waitpid( ) system call is another call that can be used to wait for child processes.

This system call however can be used to wait for a specific process to terminate.

Example:

```
#include<sys/types.h>
Pid_t wait(int *statloc);
pit_t waitpid(pid_t pid, int *status, int options);
```

The **pid** argument specifies the **PID** of the particular child process to wait for. If it is a-1 then **waitpid( )** will return information to the child process. Status information will be written to the location pointed to by status. The options argument enables us to change the behavior of waitpid( ).

A very useful option is **WNOHANG** which prevents the call to **waitpid( )** from suspending the execution of the caller. We can it to find out whether any child process has terminated and, if not, to continue. Synchronous and asynchronous process execution. In some cases,

For example: if the child process is a server or "daemon" (a process expected to run all the time in the background to deliver services such as mail forwarding) the parent process would not wait for the child to finish.

In other cases, *e.g.*, running an interactive command where it is not good design for the parent's and child's output to be mixed up into the same output stream, the parent process, *e.g.*, a shell program, would normally wait for the child to exit before continuing. If you run a shell command with an ampersand as it's last argument, *e.g.*, sleep 60 and the parent shell doesn't wait for this child process to finish.

The difference between these two functions is

- Wait can block the caller until a child process terminates, while waitpid has an option that prevents it from blocking.
- Waitpid does not wait for the first child to terminate—it has a number of options that control which process it waits for.

Exit Function

There are three ways for a process to terminate normally two forms of abnormal termination.

1. Normal termination

- executing a return from the main function. This is equivalent to calling exit.
- calling the –exit function. This function is defined by ANSI C and including the calling of all exit handlers that been registered by calling **atexit** and closing all standard I/O streams.
- calling the –exit function. This function is called by exit and handles the unix specific details.–exit is specified by POSIX.1.

2. Abnormal termination

- calling **abort.** This is a special case of the next item, since it generates the **SIGABRT** signal.
- when the process receives certain signals. The signals can be generated by the process itself. Ex.: calling **abort** function by some other process or by the kernel. **Ex.:** dividing by O.

Zombies and orphan's: They are two things happen

Child die parent active

Child active parent die.

In unix terminology the process that has terminated but whose parent has not yet waited for it, is called a **Zombie.**

Wait and Wait Pid Functions

When a process terminates, either normally or abnormally the parent is notified by the kernel sending the parent the **SIGCHLD** signal. Since, the termination of a child is an asynchronous event. This signal is the asynchronous notification from the kernel to the parent.

The process that calls **wait** or **waitpid** can

- block (if all of its children are still running).
- return immediately with the termination status of a child.
- return immediately with an error.

if the process is calling **wait** because it received the **SIGCHLD** signal, we expect wait to return immediately. But if we call it at any random point in time it can block.

pid_t wait (int * statloc):

pid_t wait pid (pid-f pid, int * statloc, int options);

Both returns: process ID if ok, 0, or –1 on error. The differences b/w these two functions are:

- wait can block the caller until a child process terminates while waitpid has an option that prevents it from blocking.
- waitpid doesn't wait for the first child to terminate—it has a number of options that control which process it waits for.

If a child has already terminated and is a zombie, wait returns immediately with that child's status. Otherwise, it blocks the caller until a child terminates. If the caller blocks and has multiple children, **wait** returns when one terminates.

exec Functions

One use of the fork function was to create a new process (the child) that then causes another program to be executed by calling one of the **exec functions**. When a process calls one of the exec functions, that process is completely replaced by the new program and the new program starts executing at its main function. The process ID does not change across an exec because a new process is not created. Exec merely replaces the current process (its text, data, heap and stack segments) with a brand new program from disk. There are six different **exec** functions, which means we could use any of the six different functions. These six functions round out the unix process control primitives.

int execl (const char *pathname, const char *argo, .../*(char*) o*/);

int execv (const char *pathname, char *const argv [ ]);

int execle (const char *pathname, const char *argo,..../*(char*) o, char* const envp[*] */);

int execve (const char *pathname, char *const argv [ ], char *cosnt envp [ ]);

int execlp (const char *filename, const char *argo, .../* (char*) o*/);

int execvp (const char *filename, char *const argv [ ]);

All six returns: –1 on error, no return on success

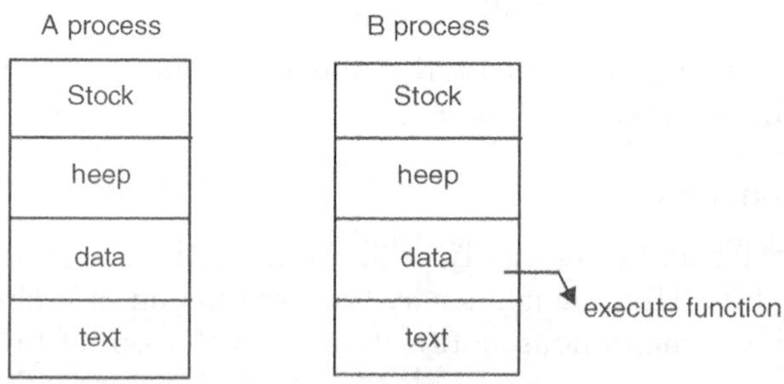

The first difference in these functions is that the first four take a pathname argument while the last two take a file name argument. When a **filename** argument is specified.

- if filename contains a slash, it is taken as a pathname.
- otherwise, the executable file is searched for in the directories specified by the **PATH** environment variable.

The **PATH** variable contains a list of directories (called path prefixes) that are separated by colons **Ex.**: The name = value environment string.

PATH = /bin: /usr/bin:/usr/local/bin/:.

Specifies **four** directories to search. If either of the two functions to **execlp** or **execvp**, finds an executable file using one of the path prefixes.

The process ID does not change after an exec, but there are additional properties that new program inherits from the calling process:

- process ID and parent process ID.
- real user ID and real group ID.
- supplementary group IDs.
- process group ID, session ID.
- controlling terminal.
- root directory file locks pending signals.
- resource limits.
- tms_utime, tms_stime, tms_cutime, and tms_ustime values

The handling of open files depends on the value of the close-on-exec flag for each descriptor.

Relationship of the six exec functions.

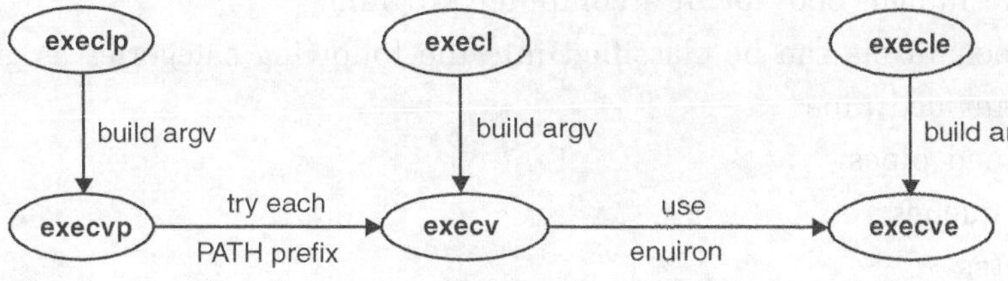

Fig. 1.9

INTER PROCESS COMMUNICATION (IPC IN UNIX)

The process of communication between each modules in a process is known as "IPC".

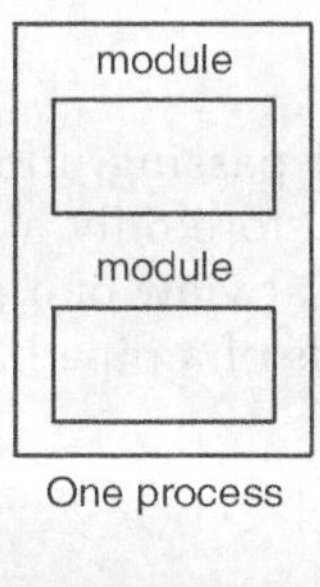

Interprocess Communication (pipes, fifos, message queues, semaphores, shared memory)

Introduction to IPC

Inter-Process Communication, which in short is known as IPC, deals mainly with the techniques and mechanisms that facilitate communication between processes. Now, why do we need special separate mechanisms or techniques for communicating between processes? Why isn't it possible to have information shared between two processes without using such special mechanisms?

Let us start from something primitive. Imagine you have two glasses completely filled with water. One glass contains hot water and the other contains cold water. What can you do to make the temperature of water in both the glasses equal? The simplest answer will be to mix the water from both the glasses in a glass with much bigger capacity. Once water is mixed, the temperature becomes equal after some time. If one can remember, this will be framed as a problem with some numerical data in a High-School Physics examination. If we go by principles, then the phenomenon here is conduction. If we go by our topic of IPC, then we can say that since the two glasses were full, we had to use another glass with a larger capacity to mix the contents in order to balance their heat energies.

Have you ever wondered about the communication medium used in telephones? What about the blood transporting system in the human body which communicates blood to different parts of the body? What about my fingers which are typing this document? My brain is doing so many things at a time. How is it directing one of my fingers to hit one key and some other fingers to hit another key? How is it synchronizing the typing work that is done by both my hands? How is it also directing me to type the letters of a word that are actually coming to my mind?

Don't worry. I am not going to give a class in Biology. But, it would be good if one can imagine a few more situations, where we are using inter-process communication, though not necessarily in the human body or in a computer program.

The IPC mechanisms can be classified into the following categories as given below:

- pipes /unnamed pipes
- fifos /named pipes
- message queues
- semaphores
- shared memory
- sockets
- signals (software interrupt)
- RPC (Remote Procedure Calls)
- Mutex and conditional variables.

Pipes

Pipes are a simple synchronized way of passing information between two processes. A pipe can be viewed as a special file that can store only a limited amount of data and uses a FIFO access scheme to retrieve data. In a logical view of a pipe, data is written to one end and read from the other. The processes on the ends of a pipe have no easy way to identify what process is on the other end of the pipe.

The system provides synchronization between the reading and writing process. It also solves the producer/consumer problem: writing to a full pipe automatically blocks, as does reading from an empty pipe. The system also assures that there are processes on both ends of the pipe at all time. The programmer is still responsible, however, for preventing deadlock between processes.

Pipes were evolved in the most primitive forms of the UNIX operating system. They provide unidirectional flow of communication between processes within the same system. In other words, they are half-duplex, which is, data flows in only one direction.

Pipes come in **two** varieties:

- **Unnamed.** Unnamed pipes can only be used by related processes (*i.e.*, a process and one of its child processes, or two of its children). Unnamed pipes cease to exist after the processes are done using them.
- **Named.** Named pipes exist as directory entries, complete with permissions. This means that they are persistent and that unrelated processes can use them.

A pipe is created by invoking the **pipe** system call, which creates a pair of **file descriptors**. These descriptors point to a pipe inode and the file descriptors are returned through the filedes argument. In the file descriptor pair, **filedes [0]** is used for reading, whereas **filedes [1]** is used for writing.

A pipe is created by calling the "pipe" function.

int pipe (int filedes [2]);

0 – on success

–1 – on error

Two file descriptors are returned through the filedes argument

filedes [0] is open for reading

filedes [1] is open for writing

The o/p of filedes [1] is the i/p for filedes [0].

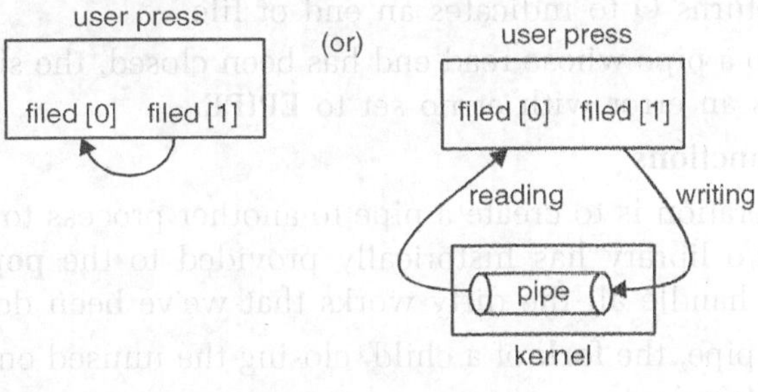

Fig. 1.10

A pipe is in a single process is next to useless. Normally, the process that calls pipe then calls **fork.** Creating on IPC CH from the parent to the child or vice versa.

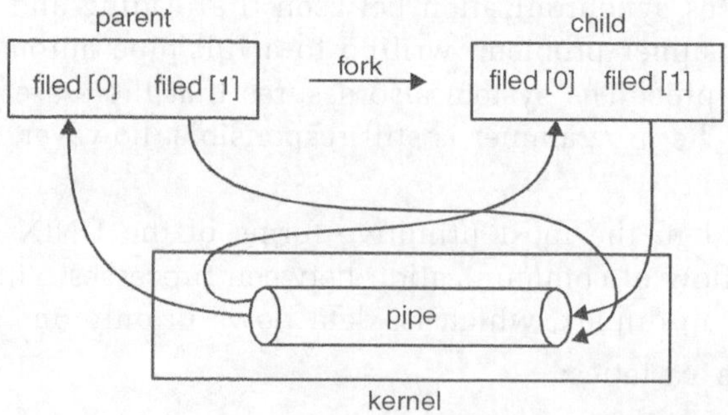

Fig. 1.11

The fork depends on which direction of data flow we want. For a **pipe** from parent to child, the parent closes the read end of the pipe filed [0] and the child closes the write end filed [1].

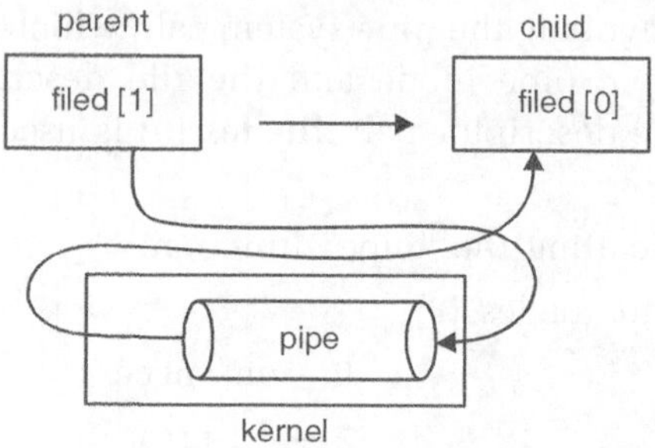

Fig. 1.12

For a pipe from the child to the parent, the parent closes filed [1] and the child closes filed [0].

When one end of pipe is closed, the following rules apply:

1. if we **read** from a pipe whose write end has been closed, after all the data has been read, read returns O to indicates an end of file.
2. if we **write** to a pipe whose read end has been closed, the signal SIGPIPE is generated. Write returns an error with errno set to **EPIPE.**

popen and pclose Functions

Since, a common operation is to create a pipe to another process to either read its o/p or send it i/p, the standard i/o library has historically provided to the **popen** and pclose functions. These two functions handle all the dirty works that we've been doing ourselves.

The creation of pipe, the **fork** of a child, closing the unused ends of the pipe and waiting for the command to terminate.

```
File *popen (const char *string, const char *type);
          Returns:  file pointer if ok
                    Null on error
int pclose (FILE *fp);
          Returns: termination status of cmdstring
                    or, -1 on error
```

The function **popen** does a fork and **exec** to execute the cmdstring and returns a standard i/o file pointer. If type is "r", the file pointer is connected to the standard o/p of cmdstring.

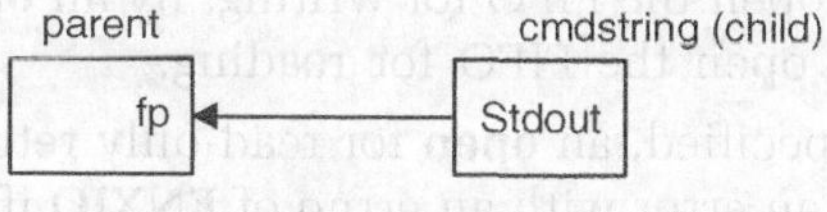

Result of fp = popen (Command "r")

If type is "w" the file pointer is connected to the standard i/p of cmdstring

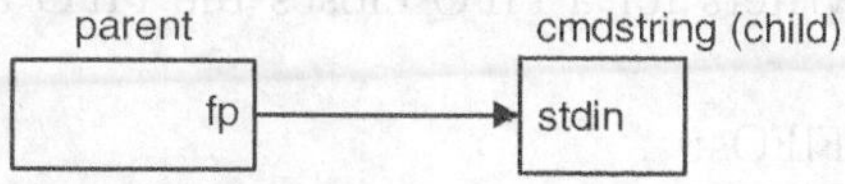

One way to remember the final argument to popen is to remember that like **fopen.** The returned file pointer is readable if type is "r", or writable if type is "w".

The pclose function closes the standard i/o stream, waits for the command to terminate and returns the termination status of the shell.

fp = popen ("ls *. c", "r");

fp = popen ("cmd 2 > 2 i", "r");

FIFOs

FIFOs are sometimes called "named pipes". Pipes can be used only b/w related process when a common ancestor has created the pipe, with FIFOs however. Unrelated processes can exchange data.

Creating a FIFO is similar to creating a file. Indead, the pathname for FIFO exists in the file system.

int mkfifo (const char *pathname, mode_t mode);

Returns: 0 if ok

−1 on error

Named Pipes (FIFOs)

A **named pipe is** a file that acts like a pipe. You put something into the file, and it comes out the other end. Thus it's called a FIFO, or First-In-First-Out: the first thing you put in the pipe is the first thing to come out the other end.

If you write to a named pipe, the process which is writing to the pipe doesn't terminate until the information being written is read from the pipe. If you read from a named pipe, the reading process waits until there's something to read before terminating. The size of the pipe is always zero — it doesn't store data, it just links two processes like the shell. However, since this pipe has a name, the two processes don't have to be on the same command line or even be run by the same user.

The specification of the mode argument for the **mkfifo** function is the same as for the **open** function. Once, we have created a FIFO using **mkfifo** we open it using open. Indeed, the normal file i/o functions (close, read, write, unlink).

When we open a FIFO, the nonblocking flag (O_NONBLOCK) affects what happens:

1. In the normal case (O_NONBLOCK not specified), an open for read only blocks until some other processes open the FIFO for writing. lly an **open** for write only blocks until some other processes open the FIFO for reading.
2. If O_NONBLOCK is specified, an **open** for read-only returns immediately. But an open for write only returns an error with an errno of **ENXIO** if no process has the FIFO open for reading.

Like a pipe, if we **write** to a FIFO that no process has open for reading the signal SIGPIPE is generated. When the lost writers for a FIFO closes the FIFO an end of file is generated for the reader of the FIFO.

There are two uses for FIFOs:

- FIFOs are used by shell commands to pass data from one shell pipeline to another. Without creating intermediate temporary files.
- **FIFOs**, are used in a client-server application to pass data b/w the clients and server.

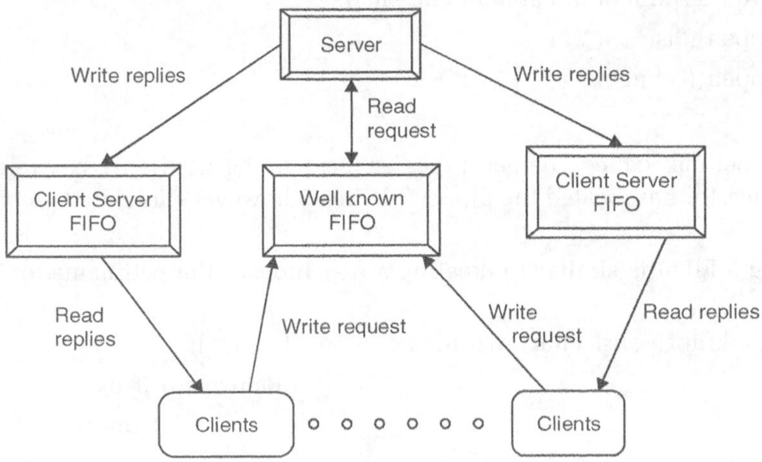

Fig. 1.13 *Client-server communication using FIFO's*

Message Queue

The basic idea of a *message queue* is a simple one.

Two (or more) processes can exchange information via access to a common system message queue. The *sending* process places via some (OS) message-passing module a message onto a queue which can be read by another process (Figure below). Each message is given an identification or type so that processes can select the appropriate message. Process must share a common key in order to gain access to the queue in the first place (subject to other permissions — see below).

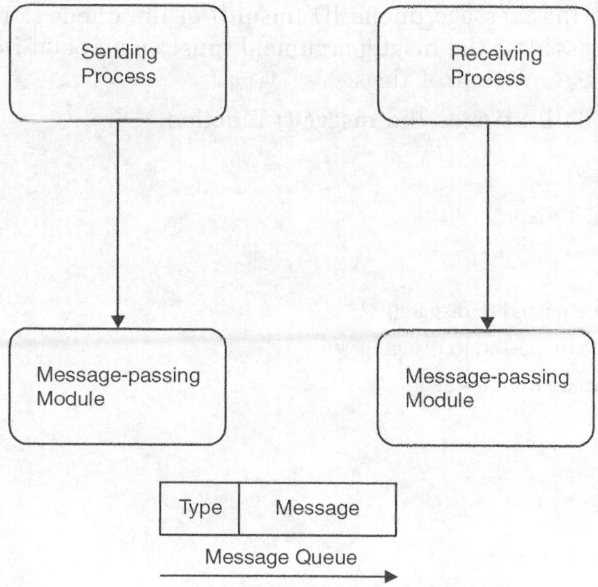

Fig. 1.14 *Basic Message Passing*

IPC messaging lets processes send and receive messages and queue messages for processing in an arbitrary order. Unlike the file byte-stream data flow of pipes, each IPC message has an explicit length. Messages can be assigned a specific type. Because of this, a server process can direct message traffic between clients on its queue by using the client process PID as the message type. For single-message transactions, multiple server processes can work in parallel on transactions sent to a shared message queue.

Before a process can send or receive a message, the queue must be initialized (through the **msgget** function see below) Operations to send and receive messages are performed by the **msgsnd( )** and **msgrcv( )** functions respectively.

When a message is sent, its text is copied to the message queue. The **msgsnd( )** and **msgrcv( )** functions can be performed as either blocking or non-blocking operations. Non-blocking operations allow for asynchronous message transfer — the process is not suspended as a result of sending or receiving a message. In blocking or synchronous message passing the sending process cannot continue until the message has been transferred or has even been acknowledged by a receiver. IPC signal and other mechanisms can be employed to implement such transfer.

A blocked message operation remains suspended until one of the following **three** conditions occurs:

- The call succeeds.
- The process receives a signal.
- The queue is removed.

Initialising the Message Queue

The **msgget( )** function initializes a new message queue:

int **msgget**(key_t key, int msgflg)

It can also return the message queue ID (**msqid**) of the queue corresponding to the key argument. The value passed as the **msgflg** argument must be an octal integer with settings for the queue's permissions and control flags.

The following code illustrates the **msgget()** function.

```
#include <sys/ipc.h>;
#include <sys/msg.h>;

...

key_t key; /* key to be passed to msgget() */
int msgflg /* msgflg to be passed to msgget() */
int msqid; /* return value from msgget() */

...

key = ...
msgflg = ...

if ((msqid = msgget(key, msgflg)) = = &ndash;1)
{
   perror("msgget: msgget failed");
   exit(1);
} else
(void) fprintf(stderr, &ldquo;msgget succeeded");
```

Controlling Message Queues

The **msgctl( )** function alters the permissions and other characteristics of a message queue. The owner or creator of a queue can change its ownership or permissions using **msgctl( )** Also, any process with permission to do so can use **msgctl( )** for control operations.

The **msgctl( )** function is prototypes as follows:

int msgctl(int msqid, int cmd, struct msqid_ds *buf)

The **msqid** argument must be the ID of an existing message queue. The cmd argument is one of:

IPC_STAT

- Place information about the status of the queue in the data structure pointed to by buf. The process must have read permission for this call to succeed.

IPC_SET

- Set the owner's user and group ID, the permissions, and the size (in number of bytes) of the message queue. A process must have the effective user ID of the owner, creator, or superuser for this call to succeed.

IPC_RMID

- Remove the message queue specified by the msqid argument.

Semaphores

Semaphores are a programming construct designed by E. W. Dijkstra in the late 1960s. Semaphores let processes query or alter status information. They are often used to monitor and control the availability of system resources such as shared memory segments.

Semaphores can be operated on as individual units or as elements in a set. A semaphore set consists of a control structure and an array of individual semaphores. A set of semaphores can contain up to 25 elements.

In a similar fashion to message queues, the semaphore set must be initialized using **semget( )**; the semaphore creator can change its ownership or permissions using **semctl()**; and semaphore operations are performed via the **semop( )** function. These are now discussed below:

Initializing a Semaphore Set

The function **semget( )** initializes or gains access to a semaphore. It is prototyped by:

int semget(key_t key, int nsems, int semflg);

When the call succeeds, it returns the semaphore **ID (semid)**.

The key argument is a access value associated with the semaphore ID.

The nsems argument specifies the number of elements in a semaphore array. The call fails when nsems is greater than the number of elements in an existing array; when the correct count is not known, supplying 0 for this argument ensures that it will succeed.

The semflg argument specifies the initial access permissions and creation control flags. The following code illustrates the semget() function.

```
#include <sys/types.h>
#include <sys/ipc.h>
#include <sys/sem.h>
...
key_t key; /* key to pass to semget() */
int semflg; /* semflg to pass tosemget() */
int nsems; /* nsems to pass to semget() */
int semid; /* return value from semget() */
..
key = ...
nsems = ...
semflg = ... ...
if ((semid = semget(key, nsems, semflg)) = = -1) {
        perror("semget: semget failed");
        exit(1); }
else
```

Controlling Semaphores

semctl( ) changes permissions and other characteristics of a semaphore set. It is prototyped as follows:

int semctl(int semid, int semnum, int cmd, union semun arg);

It must be called with a valid semaphore ID, semid. The semnum value selects a semaphore within an array by its index. The cmd argument is one of the following control flags:

GETVAL

– Return the value of a single semaphore.

SETVAL

– Set the value of a single semaphore. In this case, arg is taken as arg.val, an int.

GETPID

– Return the PID of the process that performed the last operation on the semaphore or array.

GETNCNT

– Return the number of processes waiting for the value of a semaphore to increase.

GETZCNT

– Return the number of processes waiting for the value of a particular semaphore to reach zero.

GETALL

– Return the values for all semaphores in a set. In this case, arg is taken as arg.array, a pointer to an array of unsigned shorts (see below).

SETALL

– Set values for all semaphores in a set. In this case, arg is taken as arg.array, a pointer to an array of unsigned shorts.

IPC_STAT

– Return the status information from the control structure for the semaphore set and place it in the data structure pointed to by arg.buf, a pointer to a buffer of type semid_ds.

IPC_SET

– Set the effective user and group identification and permissions. In this case, arg is taken as arg.buf.

IPC_RMID

– Remove the specified semaphore set.

A process must have an effective user identification of owner, creator, or superuser to perform an IPC_SET or IPC_RMID command. Read and write permission is required as for the other control commands. The following code illustrates semctl( ).

The fourth argument union semun arg is optional, depending upon the operation requested. If required it is of type union semun, which must be *explicitly* declared by the application program as:

```
union semun {
    int val;
    struct semid_ds *buf;
    ushort *array;
} arg;
```

```
#include <sys/types.h>
#include <sys/ipc.h>
#include <sys/sem.h>

union semun {
        int val;
        struct semid_ds *buf;
        ushort *array;
    } arg;

int i;
int semnum = ....;
int cmd = GETALL; /* get value */
i = semctl(semid, semnum, cmd, arg);
if (i == -1) {
      perror("semctl: semctl failed");
  exit(1);
}
else
...
```

Semaphore Operations

semop( ) performs operations on a semaphore set. It is prototyped by:

int **semop**(int semid, struct sembuf *sops, size_t nsops);

The **semid** argument is the semaphore ID returned by a previous semget( ) call. The sops argument is a pointer to an array of structures, each containing the following informations about a semaphore operation:

- The semaphore number
- The operation to be performed
- Control flags, if any.

The **sembuf** structure specifies a semaphore operation, as defined in <sys/sem.h>.

```
struct sembuf {
    ushort_t    sem_num;     /* semaphore number */
    short       sem_op;      /* semaphore operation */
    short       sem_flg;     /* operation flags */
};
```

The nsops argument specifies the length of the array, the maximum size of which is determined by the SEMOPM configuration option; this is the maximum number of operations allowed by a single semop( ) call, and is set to 10 by default. The operation to be performed is determined as follows:

- A positive integer increments the semaphore value by that amount.
- A negative integer decrements the semaphore value by that amount. An attempt to set a semaphore to a value less than zero fails or blocks, depending on whether IPC_NOWAIT is in effect.
- A value of zero means to wait for the semaphore value to reach zero.

There are two control flags that can be used with semop( ):

IPC_NOWAIT

– Can be set for any operations in the array. Makes the function return without changing any semaphore value if any operation for which IPC_NOWAIT is set cannot be performed. The function fails if it tries to decrement a semaphore more than its current value, or tests a nonzero semaphore to be equal to zero.

SEM_UNDO

– Allows individual operations in the array to be undone when the process exits.

This function takes a pointer, sops, to an array of semaphore operation structures. Each structure in the array contains data about an operation to perform on a semaphore. Any process with read permission can test whether a semaphore has a zero value. To increment or decrement a semaphore requires write permission. When an operation fails, none of the semaphores is altered.

The process blocks (unless the IPC_NOWAIT flag is set), and remains blocked until:

- the semaphore operations can all finish, so the call succeeds,
- the process receives a signal, or
- the semaphore set is removed.

Only one process at a time can update a semaphore. Simultaneous requests by different processes are performed in an arbitrary order. When an array of operations is given by a semop( ) call, no updates are done until all operations on the array can finish successfully. If a process with exclusive use of a semaphore terminates abnormally and fails to undo the operation or free the semaphore, the semaphore stays locked in memory in the state the process left it. To prevent this, the SEM_UNDO control flag makes semop() allocate an undo structure for each semaphore operation, which contains the operation that returns the semaphore to its previous state. If the process dies, the system applies the operations in the undo structures. This prevents an aborted process from leaving a semaphore set in an inconsistent state. If processes share access to a resource controlled by a semaphore, operations on the semaphore should not be made with SEM_UNDO in effect. If the process that currently has control of the resource terminates abnormally, the resource is presumed to be inconsistent. Another process must be able to recognize this to restore the resource to a consistent state. When performing a semaphore operation with SEM_UNDO in effect, you must also have it in effect for the call that will perform the reversing operation. When the process runs normally, the reversing operation updates the undo structure with a complementary value. This ensures that, unless the process is aborted, the values applied to the undo structure are cancel to zero. When the undo structure reaches zero, it is removed.

Sockets

A socket is a software abstraction that is used to create a channel-like interface between processes. The channel allows bi-directional communication between processes, but does little to structure the data being transmitted. In general, the serving machine in a system that uses socket communication follows several steps to initiate communication:

- Create a socket
- Map the socket to a local address
- Listen for client requests

When the client process wishes to begin a transaction with the server, it follows similar steps:

- Create a socket
- Determine the location (system name and port number) of the server
- Begin sending and/or receiving data

Types of Sockets

Communication between processes via sockets can be viewed as streams or datagram's. Stream based communication views transmitted data as a sequence of bytes, whereas datagram-based communication deals with small discrete packets of information. These packets typically contain header and trailer information in addition to the data being transmitted. Choosing a socket type is important, because each has different performance and reliability characteristics, and two communicating sockets must be of the same type.

Stream

Stream sockets are reliable; that is, data is guaranteed to be delivered in the same order it was sent. An underlying mechanism that the programmer need not be concerned with handles duplicate data, performs error checking, and controls flow. When using stream sockets, a connection is established. This means that two processes must logically agree to communicate before information can be transferred between the two of them. This connection is maintained by both processes throughout the communication session.

Datagram

Datagram sockets provide unreliable communication between the two processes, meaning that data could be received out of order. Datagram sockets provide no notion of a connection, so each datagram is sent and processed independently. This has a host of implications, one of the most significant of which is that individual datagrams can take different paths to their ultimate destination. Another important implication is that there is no flow control. Datagram packets are typically quite small and usually are fixed in sizes. No error correction is mandated, and when optional error connection is used, it is weak.

Shared Memory

Shared memory allows multiple processes to share virtual memory space so changes made by one process are instantly reflected in other processes. This affords the fastest possible IPC but is not necessarily the easiest to coordinate between the two processes. Shared memory is unique in that it allows random access of data, whereas most other IPC mechanisms mandate sequential access to data. Typically, one process creates a shared segment, and needs to set access permissions for the segment.

It is then mapped into the process's address space after the process attaches to it. Usually the creating process initializes the memory, but after this other processes that have been given access permission to the segment can use it freely. When another process does use it, it is mapped into its address space. Oftentimes semaphores are used by the original process to be sure that only one other process is allowed to access the memory at any one time, although a readers/writers lock may be a more suitable solution. When no process needs the memory segment anymore, the creating process can delete it.

Creating a Shared Memory Segment

When programming for UNIX, a new shared memory segment can be created using the **shmget( )** call.

Using **shmget( )** also generates the required data structures. If a shared memory segment was created by another process previously, using **shmget( )** allows a process to gain access to the existing segment since shared memory segments are identified by unique identifiers returned by the call. When creating a new segment, the programmer can specify a key to associate with an existing shared memory segment, the size of the segment requested, and the creation and access conditions. Note that creating a shared segment only reserves space for it; the process still cannot access it.

Controlling a Shared Memory Segment

Once a UNIX process has created a shared memory segment, it can control it using the **shmctl()** system call. This call can potentially affect existing shared memory segments as well as the system-maitained shared memory control structures. The call takes a key representing a previously created segment, a command (specified via a constant), and a buffer containing a struct that effectively serves as the parameters for the specified command. Possible commands include:

- **IPC_STAT**: returns the values of the associated data structure to a process having read access to the segment
- **IPC_SET**: allows a process with an effective UID of superuser or the UID of the process used to create the segment to modify the segment's associated user and group identifiers, as well as change the access permissions
- **IPC_RMID**: remove the system data structure, effectively indicating that the process is done with the shared segment and that if no other process is still using it then it can be deleted
- **SHM_LOCK**: allows the super user to lock a shared segment in memory
- **SHM_UNLOCK**: allows the super user to unlock a shared segment locked into memory

Shared Memory Operations

UNIX features **two** operations to work with shared memory: **shmat( ) and shmdt( ).** These allow processes to attach and detach from shared memory segments, respectively.

When a process attached to a shared memory segment using **shmat( )**, the referenced shared memory is mapped into the calling process's data segment. The call takes an identifier of an existing shared memory segment, a flag that specifies the access permissions for the shared segment and to request special conditions (such as address alignment), and a suggestion for placement of the segment. This last argument is passed in as a void*, which is usually set to null, indicating that the system should choose the addresses that it feels best. However, the process could pass in a suggested address. The memory is then mapped into the nearest available page address.

When a process wishes to detach from a segment, it can use the **shmdt( )** system call. The call takes only a reference to an attached memory segment.

❑❑❑

Unit 2

REAL-TIME SYSTEMS

Real-Time Systems: Typical real time application, Hard vs Soft real time systems,

A reference model of Real-Time Systems: Processors and resources, temporal parameters of Real-time workload, periodic task model, precedence constraints and data dependency functional parameters, Resource parameters of jobs and parameters of resources.

Commonly used approaches to Real-Time Scheduling: Clock driven, Weighted Round Robin, priority driven, Dynamic vs State Systems, Effective release times and Dead lines, offline vs online scheduling.

INTRODUCTION TO REAL-TIME OPERATING SYSTEMS

What is an RTOS?

- An RTOS is a class of operating systems that are intended for real time-applications
- What is a real time application? A real time application is an application that guarantees both correctness of result and the added constraint of meeting a deadline

So What is an RTOS?

- An operating system which follows the Real-Time criteria.
- *Efficiency, Predictability* and *Timeliness* – important
- All components of an RTOS must have these properties.
- Some tasks which may delay things:
- Interrupt Processing, Context Switching, Inter-task communication,
- IO
- To cut back on (variable) overhead for these tasks:
- Multiprogramming, Memory Management, File (and other) IO, IPC, etc.

So What Makes an RTOS Special?

- An RTOS will provide facilities to guarantee deadlines will be met
- An RTOS will provide scheduling algorithms in order to enable deterministic behaviour in the system
- An RTOS is valued more for predictability than throughput.

TYPICAL REAL-TIME APPLICATIONS

A real-time system is required to complete its work and deliver its services on a timely basis.

Example: Digital control, command and control, signal processing and telecommunication systems.

DIGITAL CONTROL

Many Real Time systems are embedded in sensors and actuators and function as digital controllers. Such system describes as follow:

- The term plant in the block diagram referes to a controlled system. Example: Engine, a brake, an aircraft, a patient.

  The state of the plant is monitored by sensors and can be changed by actuators.
- The R.T (Computing) system estimates from the sensor readings the current state of the plant and computes a control output based on the difference between the current state and the desired state (reference input). We call this computation the **control law computation** of the controller. The output thus, generated activates the actuators which bring the plant closer to the desired state.

SAMPLED DATA SYSTEMS

Long before digital computers became cost-effective and widely used, Analog (*i.e.,* continuous time and continuous-state) controlling was in use. Their principles were well estabished. Consequently, a common approach to designing a digital controller is to start with an analog controller that has the desired behaviour. The anolog version is then transformed in a digital (*i.e.,* circular run discrete-state) version. The resultant controller is a **"sampled data system".** It typically samples (*i.e.,* reads) and digitizes the anolog sensor readings periodically and carries out its control-low computation evey period. The sequence of digital outputs thus, produced is then converted back to an anolog form needed to activate the actuators.

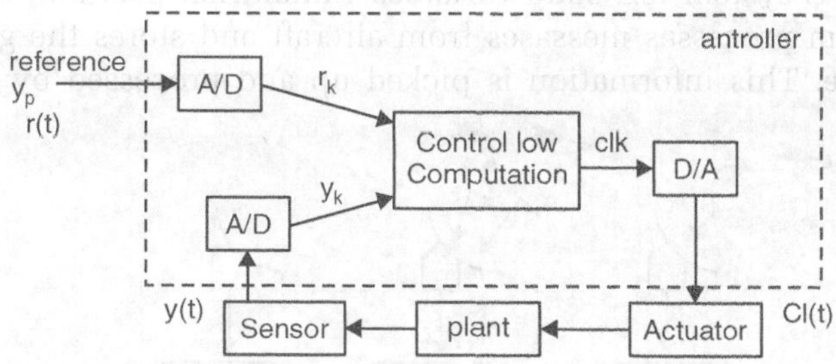

Fig. 2.1

Example: We consider an anolog-single-input (i/p)/single-output PID (proportional integral derivative) controller.

The anolog senor reading *y*(*t*) gives the measured state of the plant at time *t*. Let $e(t) = r(t) - y(t)$ denotes the difference between **desired stated *r*(*f*)**. The measured state *y*(*t*) at time *t*. The output of *u*(*t*) the controller consists of three terms:

- A term *i.e.*, proportional to *e*(*t*).
- A term *i.e.*, proportional to $\int$ of *e*(*t*).
- A term *i.e.*, proportional to derivative of *e*(*t*).

The *Yps* to the control law computation are the "sampled values" Y_k and r_k for $k = 0, 1, 2, \ldots$ which A/D convertors produce by sampling and digitizing *y*(*t*) and *r*(*t*) periodically every *T* units of time. $\boxed{e_k = r_k - y_k}$ is the *k*th sample value of *e*(*f*).

High-Level Controls

Controllers in a complex monitor and control system are typically organized hierarhically. One or more digital controllers at lowest level directly control the physical plant. Each output of a Higher-level controller is a reference input of one or more lower-level controllers.

Example of control Hierarchy ATC:

- Guidance and control
- Real-time command and control

The controller at the highest level of a control hierarchy is a command and control system. An ATC system is an excellent example. Figure shows architecture of ATC.

ATC system monitors the aircrast in its coverage area and environmentor weather condition and generates and presents the information needed by the operators *i.e.*, (ATC's). outputs from the ATC system include the assigned arrival times to metering fixes for individual aircraft. As stated earlier. These output's are reference input's to on-boord flight management system.

Thus, the ATC system indirectly controls the embedded components in low levels of the control hierarchy in addition, the ATC system provides voice and telemetry links to on-board allionics. Thus, it support the comm. among the operatros at both levels *i.e.*, (pilots and airtraffic controllers).

The ACT system gather information on the state of each aircarft via one or more active Radars. Such a radar interrogates each aircraft periodically. When interrogated, an craft responds by sending to the ATC system its "state variables": identifier, position, altitude, heading, and soon. The ACT system processes messases from aircraft and stores the gate information thus, obtained in data base. This information is picked up and processed by display processors.

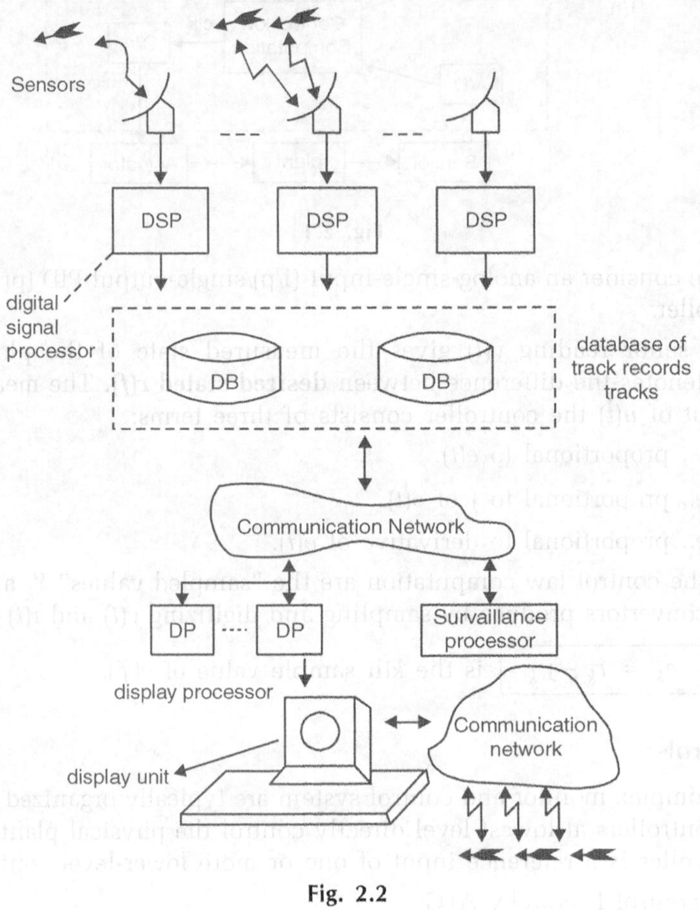

Fig. 2.2

SIGNAL PROCESSING

Most signal-processing applications have some kind of real-time requirements.

- Processing between Demands

Radar System

A signal processing application is typically a part of a larger system. Figure shows a block diagram of a (passive) radar signal processing and tracking system.

- The system consists of an I/O sub-system that samples and digitizes the echo signal from the radar and places the sampled values in a shared memory.

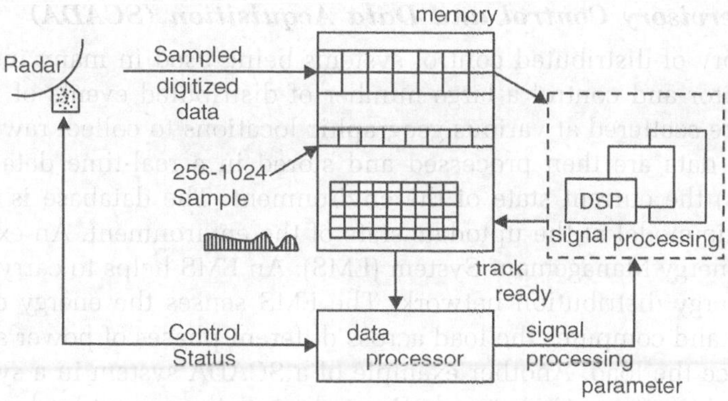

Fig. 2.3

REAL-TIME APPLICATIONS

Digital control, optional control, command and control signal processing and tracking, real-time data base and multimedia.

Applications of Real-Time Systems

Real-time systems have of late, found applications in wide ranging areas. In the following, we list some of the prominent areas of application of real-time systems and in each identified case, we discuss a few example applications in some details. As we can imagine, the list would become very vast if we try to exhaustively list all areas of applications of real-time systems. We have therefore restricted our list to only a handful of areas, and out of these we have explained only a few selected applications to conserve space. We have pointed out the quantitative notions.

Industrial Applications: Industrial applications constitute a major usage area of real-time systems. A few examples of industrial applications of real-time systems are: process control systems, industrial automation systems, SCADA applications, test and measurement equipments, and robotic equipments.

Example 1: Chemical Plant Control

Chemical plant control systems are essentially a type of process control application. In an automated chemical plant, a real-time computer periodically monitors plant conditions. The plant conditions are determined based on current readings of pressure, temperature and chemical concentration of the reaction chamber. These parameters are sampled periodically. Based on the values sampled at any time, the automation system decides on the corrective actions necessary at that instant to maintain the chemical reaction at a certain rate. Each time the plant conditions are sampled the automation system should decide on the exact instantaneous corrective actions required such as changing the pressure, temperature, or chemical concentration and carry out these actions within certain predefined time bounds. Typically, the time bounds in such a chemical plant control application range from a few micro seconds to several milli seconds.

Example 2: Supervisory Control and Data Acquisition (SCADA)

SCADA is a category of distributed control systems being used in many industries. A SCADA system helps monitor and control a large number of distributed events of interest. In SCADA systems, sensors are scattered at various geographic locations to collect raw data (called events of interest). These data are then processed and stored in a real-time database. The database models (or reflects) the current state of the environment. The database is updated frequently to make it a realistic model of the uptodate state of the environment. An example of a SCADA application is an Energy Management System (EMS). An EMS helps to carry out load balancing in an electrical energy distribution network. The EMS senses the energy consumption at the distribution points and computes the load across different phases of power supply. It also helps dynamically balance the load. Another example of a SCADA system in a system that monitors and controls traffic in a computer network. Depending on the sensed load in different segments of the network, the SCADA system makes the router change its traffic routing policy dynamically. The time constraint in such a SCADA application is that the sensors must sense the system state at regular intervals (say every few milli seconds) and the same must be processed before the next state is sensed.

Example 3: Medical: A few examples of medical applications of real-time systems are: robots, MRI scanners, radiation therapy equipments, bedside monitors and computerized axial tomography (CAT).

Example 4: Robot Used in Recovery of Displaced Radioactive Material

Robots have become very popular nowadays and are being used in a wide variety of medical applications. An application that we discuss here is a robot used in retrieving displaced radioactive materials. Radioactive materials such as Cobalt and Radium are used for treatment of cancer. At times during treatment, the radioactive Cobalt (or Radium) gets dislocated and falls down. Since, human beings can not come neat a radioactive material, a robot is used to restore the radioactive material to its proper position. The robot walks into the room containing the radioactive material, picks it up, and restores it to its proper position. The robot has to sense its environment frequently and based on this information, plan its path. The real-time constraint on the path planning task of the robot is that unless it plans the path fast enough after an obstacle is detected, it may collide with it. The time constraints involved here are of the order of a few milli seconds.

Peripheral equipments: A few examples of peripheral equipments that contain embedded real-time systems are: laser printers, digital copiers, fax machines, digital cameras and scanners.

Example 5: Laser Printer: Most laser printers have powerful microprocessors embedded in them to control different activities associated with printing. The important activities that a microprocessor embedded in a laser printer performs include the following: getting data from the communication port(s), typesetting fonts, sensing paper jams, noticing when the printer runs out of paper, sensing when the user presses a button on the control panel, and displaying various messages to the user. The most complex activity that the microprocessor performs is driving the laser engine. The basic command that a laser engine supports is to put a black dot on the paper. However, the laser engine has no idea about the exact shapes of different fonts, font sizes, italic, underlining, boldface, etc. that it may be asked to print. The embedded microprocessor receives print commands on its input port and determines how the dots can be composed to achieve the desired document and manages printing the exact shapes through a series of dot commands issued to the laser engine. The time constraints involved here are of the order of a few milli seconds.

Example 6: A Cellular System: Cellular systems have become a very popular means of mobile communication. A cellular in the cell. Besides, the base of station performs several tasks such as locating a user, sending and receiving control message to a handset, keeping track of of call details for billing purposes, and hand-off of calls as the mobile moves. Call hand-off is required when a mobile moves away from a base station. As a mobile moves away, its received signal strength (RSS) fall at the base station. The base station monitors this and as soon as the RSS falls below a certain threshold value, it hand-off the details of the on-going call of the mobile to the base station of the cell to which the mobile has moved. The hand-off must be completed within a sufficiently small predefined time interval, so that the user does not feel any temporary disruption of service during the hand-off. Typical call band-off is required to be achieved within a few milliseconds.

Aerospace: A few important uses of real-time systems in aerospace applications are: avionics, flight simulation, airline cabin management systems, satellite tracking systems and computer on-board an aircraft.

Example 7: Railway Reservation System

In a railway reservation system, a central repository maintains the up-to-date data on booking status of various trains. Ticket booking counters are distributed across different geographic locations. Customers queue up at different booking counters and submit their reservation requests. After a reservation request is made at a counter, it normally takes only a few seconds for the system to confirm the reservation and print the ticket. A real-time constraint in this application is that once a request is made to the computer, it must print the ticket or display the seat unavailability message before the average human response time (about 20 seconds) expires, so that the customers do not notice any delay and get a feeling of having obtained instant results. However, as we discuss a little later (in Sec. 1.6), this application is an example of a category of applications that is in some aspects different from the other discussed applications. For example, even if the results are produced just after 20 Secs, nothing untoward is going to happen—this may not be the case with the other discussed applications.

OTHER REAL-TIME APPLICATIONS

- Real-time data bases
  - ↳ Absolute Temporal consistency
  - ↳ Relative Temporal consistency
  - ↳ Consistency models
- Multimedia applications
  - ↳ MPEG Compression/Decompression
    - ↳ Motion estimation
    - ↳ DCT and Encoding
    - ↳ Decompression
    - ↳ Real-time characteristics

Hard vs Soft Real-Time Systems

JOBS AND PROCESSORS

For the purpose of describing and characterizing different types of real-time systems-methods for scheduling and resource management, it is more convenient for us to speak all kinds of work done by computing and communicate systems in general terms. We call each unit of work *i.e.,* scheduled and executed by the system **"a Job"** and a set of related Jobs which Jointly provide some system fun's a **"task"**. Hence, the computation of a control law is a Job. So is the computation of a FFT of sensor data on the Txion of a data packet, or the retrieval of a file and so on.

Similarly, rather than using different verbs (Example, Compute and transmit) for different types of Jobs. We say that a Job execute or is executed by the system. Every Job executes on some resources. For example, the Jobs mentioned above execute on a CPU, a network and a disk respectively. These resources are called servers in queuing theory. Literature and sometimes, active resources in real-time system literature. To avoid overloading this term, we call all these resources "processors" except occasionally.

RELEASE TIMES, DEADLINES AND TIMING CONSTRAINTS

The **release time** of a Job is the instant of time at which the Job becomes available for execution. The Job can be scheduled and executed at any time at or after its release time whenever its data and control dependency conditions are met.

Example, we consider a system which monitors and controls several furnances. After it is initialized and starts execution (say at time 0) the system samples and reads each temperature sensor every 100 msec and places the sampled reading in memory. We say that Jobs have no release time if all the jobs are released when the system being execution.

The deadline of a job is the instant at time by which its execution is required to be completed.

Example, their deadlines are 120 msec, 220 msec, and so on, respectively. Alternatively, if the control-law computation Jobs must complete sooner, their deadlines may be 70 msec, 170 msec so on, we say that job has no deadline if its deadline is at infinity.

- The length of time from the release time of the job to the instant when it completes. We call the maximum allowable response time of a job its **"relative deadline"**.
- The deadline of a Job, sometimes called its **"absolute deadline"** is equal to its **release time** plus its **relative deadline.**
- We call a constraint imposed on the timing behaviour of a job a "timing constraint". In its simplest form a timing constraint of a job can be specified in terms of its release time and relative or absolute deadlines.

It is commonly divide timing constraints into two types.

Hard soft timing constraints.

COMMON DEFINITIONS

According to a commonly used definition, a timing constraint or deadline is **hard** if the failure to meet it is considered to be a **fatal** fault. A hard deadline is imposed on a Job because a late result produced by the Job after the deadline may have disastrous consequences.

Example: A late command to stop a train may cause a collision. In contrast, the late completion of a Job that has a soft deadline is undesirable. However, a few misses of soft deadline do not serious harm; only the system overall performance becomes poorer and poorer when more and more Jobs with soft deadlines complete late.

In real time system's, the distinction between the **hard** and **soft** timing constraints is sometimes stated quantitatively in terms of the usefulness of results (therefore the overall system performance) as function of the **"tardinesses"** of jobs. The **tardiness** of a job measures how late it completes respective to its deadline. Its tardiness is zero if the Job completes at or before its deadline. Otherwise, if the Job is late its tardiness is equal to the difference between its completion time (*i.e.*, the time instant at which it completes execution) and its deadline.

The usefulness of a result produced by a soft real-time Job (*i.e.*, a Job with a soft deadline) decreases gradually as the tarding of the Job ↑8.

The usefulness of a result produced by a hard real-time Job falls off abruptly and may even become –ve when the tardiness of the Job becomes larger than zero.

The deadline of Job is softer if the usefulness of its result ↓ at a slower rate.

HARD TIMING CONSTRAINTS AND TEMPORAL QUALITY OF SERVICE GUARANTEES

The timing constraint of a Job is hard, and the job is a hard real-time Job, if the user requires the validation that the system always meet the timing constraint. By validation, we mean a demonstration by a provably correct, efficient procedure and by exhaustive simulation and testing.

On the other hand, if no **validation** is required, or only a demonstration that the Job meet some **"statistical constraints"** (*i.e.*, a timing constraint specified in terms of statistical averages suffices, then the timing constraint of the Job is soft.

We differentiate between hard and soft timing constraints is compatible with the distinction between **guaranteed** and **best-effort** services. States another way, if the user wants the temporal quality (Example, response time and jitter) of the service provided by a task guaranteed and the satisfaction of the timing constraints defining the temporal quality volidated. Then the timing constraints are hard.

We call an application (task) with hard timing constraints a hard real-time application and a system containing mostly hard real-time applications a hard real-time system.

Example: digital controllers, all the tasks and jobs execute in every operation mode of the system are known a priori.

HARD REAL-TIME SYSTEMS

The requirement that all hard timing constraints must be validated invariably places many restrictions on the design and implementation or hard-real time applications as well as on the architecte of H/w and system s/w used to support them.

Some Reasons for Requiring

Many E.S are hard real-time system deadlines of job in an E.S are typically derived from the required responsiveness of the sensors and actuators monitored and controlled by it.

Example: We consider an automatically controlled train. It can't stop instantaneously. When the signal is red (stop) its braking action must be activated a certain distance away from the signal post at which the train must stop. This braking distance depends on the speed of the train and the safe value of decleration. From the speed and safe decleration of the train. The controller can compute the time for the train to travel the braking distance. This time in turn imposes a constraint on the response time of Jobs which sense and process the stop signal and activate the brake.

Each control-law computation Job of a flight controller must be completed in time so that its command can be issued in time. Otherwise, the plane controlled by it may become oscillatory or even unstable and uncontrollable. For this reason, we want the timely completion of all control-law computations **guaranteed.** Example, NAVSTAR system is (GPS) more complex one, the effect of missed deadlines may be combined with other factors in ways impossible to predict. Consequently, the designer makes sure that the system misses no deadline as long as it is in operation. The hard real-time requirement in fact simplifies the process of validating the overall system designer building system.

More on Hard-Timing Constraints

- deterministic constraints: more used in hard realine constantly in this only.
- probabilistic constraints.
- constraint: in terms of some usefulness functions.

SOFT REAL-TIME SYSTEM

As system in which Jobs have soft deadlines is a "soft real-time system". The developer of a soft real-time system is rarely required to prove rigorously that the system surely meet its real-time performance objective.

Example: On-line transaction systems and telephone switches as well as electronic games.

A system may have critical timing requirements but is nevertheless considered to be a soft real-time system. An **example** is a stock price quotation system it should update the price of each stock each time the price changes.

The timing requirements of soft real time systems are often specified in probabilistic terms.

Example: telephone N/w explain.

As a final **example.** Let us consider **multimedia system** that provide the user with services of "guaranteed" quality.

Example: A frame of a movie must be delivered every 30th of a second and difference in the times when each video frame is displayed and when the accompanied speech is presented should be no more than 80 msec.

The quality of service guarantee is soft the validation requirement is soft and the timing constraints defining the quality are soft.

PROCESSORS AND RESOURCES

We divide all the system resources into two motor types:

- processors
- resources

Processors are often called **servers** and **active resources:** Computers, Txion links, disks and database servers are examples of processors. They carry out machine instructions, move data from one place to another, retrieve files, process queries and so on.

Sometimes we distinguish the **type's** of processors. Two processors are of the same type if they are functionally identical and can be used interchangeably. Hence, two Txion links with the same Txion rate between a pair of Sender and Receiver are processors of the same type Example, SMP (Symetrical Multiprocessor) processors that are functionally different or for some other reason can't be used interchangeably are of different types CPUs, Txion links and disks are of different types because they are functionally different. A Txion link connecting an on-board flight management system to the GND controller is a different types of processor from the link connecting two air traffic control centers even when the links have the same characteristics, because they can't be used interchangeably.

The letter *P* to denote processor (s). When we want focus on how the Jobs on each processor are, scheduled how the Jobs on different processors are synchronized. If we consider *m* processors then in the system P_1, P_2 ..... P_m.

By **resources,** we will specifically mean **"passive designing".**

Example: Memory, sequence no's, mutexes data base locks. A Job may need some resources in addition to the processor in order to make progress.

One of the attributes of a processor is its **speed.**

Example: We consider a data link that uses the **sliding-window** scheme to regulate message Txion. Only maximum number of messages are allowed to be in transit. /*Write own*/.

We will use the letter ***R*** to denote **resources.** The resources in the examples mentioned above are reusable.

Example: Let us consider the I/O bus. Every computation Job must have the I/O bus in addition to the processor to execute. Most of the time, we model the I/O bus as a resource, often times a plentiful and therefore ignored resources. However, when we want to study how long I/O activities may delay the completion of computation Jobs that share the I/O bus or when we want to determine the real-time performance of an I/O bus arbitration scheme, we want to model the bus as a resource or a processor.

TEMPORAL PARAMETERS OF REAL-TIME WORKLOAD

The workload on processor consists of Jobs, each of which is a unit of work to be allocated processors time and other resources. A set of related Jobs that execute to support a function of the system is a task. In many E.S, the number of tasks is fixed as long as the system remains in an operation mode. The number of tasks may change when the system operation mode changes, and the number of tasks in the new mode is also known. Example, **flight control system.**

In some other systems the number of tasks may change as tasks are added and deleted while the system executes.

Example: In on ATC system each surveillance task monitors an aircraft. The number of such tasks changes as tasks are added and deleted when aircraft enters and leaves the coverage area.

Each Job J_i is characterized by its temporal parameters:

- functional parameters
- resource parameters
- interconnection parameters.
- Its temporal parameters tell us its timing constraints behaviour.
- Its interconnection parameters describes how it depends on other Jobs and how other Jobs depend on it.
- Its functional parameters specify the intrinsic properties of the Job.
- Its resource parameters gives us its resource requirements.
- Release time, absolute deadline and relative deadline of a Job J_i, These are temporal parameters. We will use r_i, d_i, and D_i respectively to denote them and call the time interval $(r_i, d_i]$ between release time and absolute deadline of the Job J_i its **feasible interval,** we consider these parameters to be parts of the system specification.

FIXED-JITTERED AND SPORADIC RELEASE TIMES

We do not know exactly when each Job will be released. In other word, the actual **release time** r_i of each **Job J_i**. Only that r_i is in a range $[r_i^-, r_i^+]$. r_i can be as early as the earliest release time r_i^- and as late as the latest release time r_i^+. Indeed some models assume that only the range of r_i is known and coll this range the **Jitter** in r_i or **release-time Jitter**. Sometimes, the Jitter is negligibly small compared with the values of other temporal parameters. If for practical purposes, we can approximate the actual release time of each Job by its earliest or latest release time, then we say that the Job has a **fixed** release time.

Almost every real-time system is required respond to external events which occur at random instants of time. When such an event occurs, the system executes a set of Jobs in response. The release times of these Jobs are not known until the event triggering them occurs. These Jobs are called "sporiadie or aperiodic Jobs" be's they are released at random time instants.

Example: The pilot may disengage (separate, release or detach) remove the autopilot system at anytime. When this occurs. The autopilot system changes from cruise mode to standby mode. The Jobs that execute to accomplish this mode change are sporadic Jobs.

The release times of sporadic and aperiodic Jobs are random variables. The model of the system gives the probability distribution $A(x)$ of the release time of such a Job. The term **arrival times** (or interarrival time) which is commonly used in **Queueing Theory**. An aperiodic Job arrives when it is released. $A(x)$ is the arrival time distribution (or interarrival time distribution).

EXECUTION TIME (e_i)

Another temporal parameter of a Job. J_i is its execution time e_i. e_i is the amount of time required to complete the execution of J_i when it executes alone and has all the resources it requires. Hence, the value of this parameter depends mainly on the complexity of the Job and the speed of the processor used to execute the Job, not on how the Job is scheduled.

The actual amount of time required by Job to complete its execution may vary for many reasons.

Example: A computation may contain conditional branches, and these conditional branches may take different amounts of time to complete. The branches taken during the execution of the computation Job depend on the input data.

We know that the execution time of the job $[e_i^-, e_i^+]$, where e_i^- and e_i^+ are the minimum execution times. The maximum execution time of Job J_i. We usually assume that we know e_i^- and e_i^+ of every hard real-time Job J_i, but the actual execution time of the Job is unknown.

For the purpose of determining whether each Job can always complete by its deadline knowing the maximum execution time of each Job often suffices. The term e_i of each Job J_i specifically means its maximum e_i. In some systems the responge times of some Jobs may be larger when the actual execution times of some Jobs are smaller than their maximum values in these cases, we will have to deal with the variations in execution times explicitly.

However, there are **two good reasons** for the common use of the **deterministic approach.**

- Many Hard-real time systems are safety-critical. These systems are typically designed and implemented in a such way that the variations in Job execution times are kept as small as possible. The need to have relatively deterministic execution times places many restrictions on implementation choices. By working with these restrictions and making the execution times of Jobs almost deterministic.

- The other reason for the common use of the deterministic approach is that the hard-real time portion of the system is often small. The timing requirements of the rest of the system are soft. We can then use the methods and tools supported by the deterministic models to ensure that the hard-timing constraints will surely be met at all times.

PERIODIC TASK MODEL

The periodic task model is a well-known deterministic work load model. With its various extensions, the model characterizes accurately many traditional hard real-time applications, such as digital control, real-time monitoring and constant bit-rate voice/video Txion.

Periods, Execution Times and Phases of Periodic Tasks

In the periodic task model, each computation (or) data Txion *i.e.,* executed repeatly at regular or semi regular time intervals in order to provide a function, of the system on a continuing basis is modeled as a **period task.** Specifically each periodic task, **denoted by T_i,** is a sequence of Jobs.

- The **period P_i** of the T_i is the minimum length of all time intervals between release times of consecutive Jobs in T_i.
- **Its execution time** is the maximum e_i of all the Jobs in it. At all times, the period and execution time of every periodic task in the system are known.
- The term periodic task refers to a task *i.e.,* truly periodic *i.e.,* interrelease times of all Jobs in a periodic task are equal to its period.
- The accuracy of the periodic task model decreasing with increasing Jitter in release times and variations in execution times. So, a periodic task is an inaccurate model of the Txion of a variable bitrate video, because of the large variations in the e_i's of Jobs. A periodic task is also an inaccurate model the Txion of cells on a real-time connection through a switched N/w that does not do traffic shapping at every switch because large release time Jitters are possible.

We call the tasks in the system T_1, T_2 in necessary to safer to the individual Jobs in a task T_i, we call them $J_{i,1}$, $J_{i,2}$ and so on J_i, k being the kth Job in T_i, we also call individual Jobs J_1, J_2, ..., J_n.

The release time $r_{i,1}$ of the first Job $J_{i,1}$ in each task T_i is called the "ϕ of T_i". *i.e.,* $\phi_i = r_{i,1}$. In general, different tasks may have different phases. Some tasks are **in phase** meaning that they have the same phase.

We use H to denote the least common multiple of P_i for i = 1, 2, ... n. A time interval of length H is called a **hyperperiod** of the T_i. The maximum number N of Jobs in each hyperperiod is equal to $\sum_{i=1}^{n} \frac{H}{P_i}$. The length of a H of **three** T_i with P_i 3, 4 and 10 is 60. The total number N of Jobs in the H is 41.

We call the ratio $u_i = e_i/p_i$ the **utilization of task** T_i. u_i is equal to the fraction of time a truly T_i with P_i and e_i keeps a processor busy. The **total utilization** U of all the tasks in the system is the sum of the utilizations of the individual tasks in it.

APERIODIC AND SPORADIC TASKS

That a real time system is invariably required to respond to external events to respond it executes aperiodic or sporadic Jobs whose release times are not known a priori. An operator is adjustment of the sensitivity setting of a radar surveillance system is an example.

PRECEDENCE CONSTRAINTS AND DATA DEPENDENCY

Data and control dependencies among Jobs may constrains the order in which they can execute. In classical scheduling theory the Jobs are said to have precedence constraints. If they are constrained to execute in some order. Otherwise, if the Jobs can execute in any order. They are said to independent.

Example: In a radar surveillance system the signal-processing task is the producer of track records, while the tracker task is the consumer. In particular, each tracker Job processes the track records generated by a signal-processing Job. The designer may choose to synchronize the tasks so that the execution of the kth tracker Job does not begin until the kth signal-processing Job completes. The tracker Job is precedence constrained.

Example: We consider queries to an information server.

PRECEDENCE GRAPH AND TASK GRAPH

We use a partial order relation < called a **precedence relation** over the set of Jobs to specify the precedence constraints among Jobs. A Job J_i **is a predecessor** of another Job J_k (and J_k a successor of J_i) if J_k can't begin execution until the execution of J_i completes. A short-hand notation to state this fact is $J_i < J_k$. J_i is an **immediate predecessor** of J_k and J_k is an immediate successor of J_i. If $J_i < J_k$ and there is no other Job J_j such that $J_i < J_j < J_k$. Two Jobs J_i and J_k are independent when neither $J_i < J_k$ nor $J_k < J_i$.

A classical way to represent the precedence constraints among Jobs in a set J is by a directed graph $G = (J, <)$. Each vertex in this graph represents a Job in J. We will call each vertex by the name of the Job represented by it. There is a directed edge from the vertex J_i to the vertex. J_k when the Job J_i is an immediate predecessor of the Job J_k. This graph is called a **precedence graph.**

A **task graph,** which gives as a general way to describe the application system is an extended precedence graph. Figure shows a task graph. As in a precedence graph. The vertices in a task graph represent Jobs. They are shown as circles and squares in this figure.

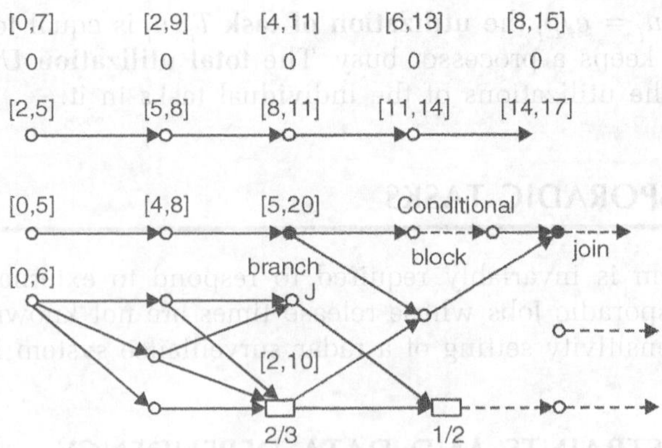

Fig. 2.4

Specifically, the system described by the graph in figure includes two periodic tasks. The task whose Job are represented by the vertices in the top row has phase O, period 2 and relative deadline 7. The Jobs in it are independent; there are no edges to or from these Jobs.

The vertices in the second row represent Jobs in a periodic task with phase 2, period 3 and relative deadline 3. The Jobs in it are dependent: the Ist Job is the immediate predecessor of the 2nd Job. The 2nd Job is the immediate predecessor of the 3rd Job and so on. The precedence graph of this task is a chain as shown here. A subgraph's being **a chain** indicates that for every pair of Jobs J_i and J_k in the subgraph either $J_i < J_k$ or $J_i > J_k$. Hence, the Jobs must be executed in serial order. The precedence graph a task graph may contain different types of edges that represents different types of dependencies. The type(s) of dependency represented by an edge is given by the types(s) of the edges. The types of an edge connecting two vertices and other parameters of the edge are **interconnection** parameters of the Jobs represented by the vertices.

Data Dependency

Data dependency can't be captured by a precedence graph. In many real time systems, Jobs communicate via shared data. oftentimes, the designer chooses not to synchronize producer and consumer Jobs. Rather, each producer places the data generated by it in a shared address space to be used by the consumerat any time. In this case, the closical precedence graph should show that the producer and consumer are independent because they are not explicitly constrained to execute inturn.

Example: In an avionics system, the navigation Job updates the location of the airplane periodically. These data are placed in shared space. Whenever the flight management Job needs navigation data, it reads the most current data produced by the navigation Job. There is no precedence constraint between the navigation Job and the flight management Job.

In a task graph, data dependencies among Jobs are repregented explicitly by data dependency edges among Jobs. There is a data dependency edge from a vertex J_i to vertex J_k in the task graph of the Job. J_k consumes data generated by J_i or the Job J_i sends messages to J_k. A parameter of an edge from J_i to J_k is the volume of data from J_i to J_k.

Functional Parameters

While scheduling and resource access-control decisions are made disregarding most functional characteristics of Jobs, several functional properties do affect these decisions. Among them are

→ Preemptivity → Criticality → Optional interval → Laxity type and laxityfunction

Data Dependency

- In many Real time system jobs communicate with shared data.
- There is a data dependency edge from a vertix J_i to vertix J_k in the task graph.
- If the job J_k consumes data generated by J_i loss the job J_i sends message to J_k.
- A parameter of an edge from j_i to j_k is the volume of data froms J_i to J_k.

Functional Parameters

Functional parameters are preemptivity of jobs, criticality of jobs, optional executives and laxity type.

PREEMPTIVITY OF JOBS

- The scheduler may suspend the execution of a less urgent job and give the processor to move urgent job.
- The interruption of job execution is called **"preemption"**.
- If job is preemptable, its execution can suspend at any time to allow the execution of other jobs.
- In non-Real time system such jobs are typically scheduled is a round-robin manner. This is possible become they are preemptable.
- If the job is non-preemptable if it is evented from start to completion without any interruption.
- If a job is non preemptable if it is treated as constraint of the job.

CRITICALITY OF JOBS

- The importance of a job is +ve number that indicates how critical the job is w.r.t other jobs.
- In this criticality of jobs priority and weight are others used to refer to importance.

Example: In flight control management system the job that controls the flight of the aircraft is more critical than the navigation job.

OPTIONAL EXECUTION

Laxity Type and Laxity Function

- Laxity type of job indicates whether its timing constraints we just Head.

- Laxity type of a job is sometimes supplemented by a usefulness of unit.

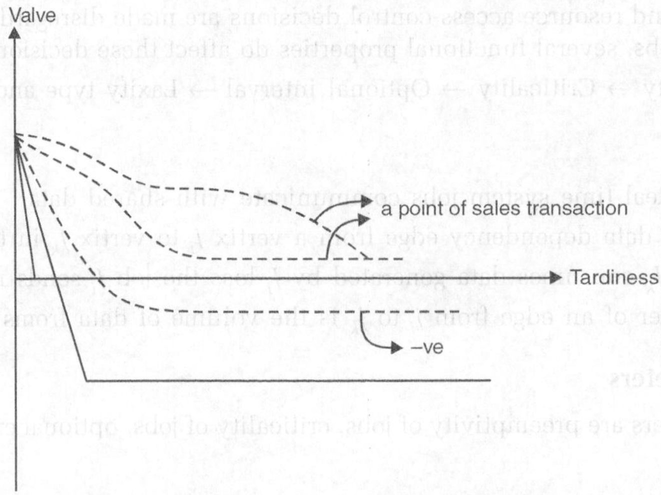

Fig. 2.5. *Example of usefulness function.*

- Function gives the usefulness of the result produced by the job as function of its **'tardiness'**.
- Solid step functions are usually associated with hard real-time jobs.
- The usefulness of the result becomes zero or negative as soon as the job is tardy.
- The Transmission and execution of a command to release a bomb on a target is an example of jobs with this laxity type.
- We can use these usefulness functions to describe qualitatively the real-time performance objectives of the system.

Resource Parameters of Jobs and Parameters of Resources

- Every job requires a processor throughout its execution. In addition processor job may also require some resources.

Preemptivity of Resources

- A resource parameter is preemptivity.
- A resource is non-preemptable if each unit of the resource is constrained to be used serially.
- Non-preemptivity is a property of the token ring.
- Transmission of a message over a taken ring, it interrpted, must be reduce from the beginning is a consequence of the way the medium access protocol works.
- Message transmission jobs are, in fact preemptable.

Resource graph

- In a resource graph, there is a vertex R_i for every processor or Resource R_i in the system.

- Edges in task graphs represent different types of dependencies.
- Edges in a resource graph represent the relationship among resources.
- An Edge from a vertex R_i to another vertex R_k can mean that R_k is a component of R_i.
- Some edges in resources graphs represent connectivity between components. These edges are called **"accessibility edges"**.

COMMONLY USED APPROACHES TO REAL-TIME SCHEDULING

Introduction

Several schemes of classification of real-time task scheduling algorithms exist. A popular scheme classifies the real-time task scheduling algorithms based on how the scheduling points are defined. The three main types of schedules according to this classification scheme are: clock-driven, event-driven and hybrid.

> The clock-driven schedulers are those in which the scheduling points are determined by the interrupts received from a clock. In the even-driven ones, the scheduling points are defined by certain events which precludes clock interrupts. The hybrid ones use both clock interrupts as well as event occurrences to define their scheduling points.

A few important members of each of these three broad classes of scheduling algorithms are the following:

1. Clock Driven:
   - Table-driven
   - Cyclic
2. Event Driven:
   - Simple priority-based
   - Rate Monotonic Analysis (RMA)
   - Earliest Deadline First (EDF)
3. Hybrid:
   - Round-robin.

Important members of clock-driven schedulers that we discuss in this text are table-driven and cyclic schedulers. Clock-driven schedulers are simple and efficient. Therefore, these are frequently used in embedded applications. Important examples of event-driven schedulers are Earliest Deadline First (EDF) and Rate Monotonic Analysis (RMA). Event-driven schedulers are more sophisticated than clock-driven schedulers and usually are more proficient and flexible than clock-driven schedulers. These are more proficient because they can feasibly schedule some task sets which clock-driven schedulers cannot. These are more flexible because they can feasibly schedule sporadic and aperiodic tasks in addition to periodic tasks, whereas clock-driven schedulers can satisfactorily handle only periodic tasks. Event-driven scheduling of real-time tasks in a uniprocessor environment was a subject of intense research during early 1970's, leading to publication of a large number of research results. Out of the large number of research results that were published, the following two popular algorithms are the essence of all those results: Earliest Deadline First (EDF), and Rate Monotonic Analysis (RMA). If we understand these two schedulers well, we would get a good grip on real-time task scheduling on uniprocessors. Several variations to these two basic algorithms exist.

Scheduling Issues

- Scheduling of independent periodic tasks.
- Scheduling of dependent tasks.
- Scheduling with dynamic priority assignment.
- Hybrid task set scheduling.
- Scheduling schemes for handling overload.
- Multiprocessor scheduling.
- Joint scheduling of tasks and messages in distributed systems.

Clock-Driven Approach

- As the name implies when scheduling is clock-driven (also called time driven) decisions on what jobs execute at what times are made at specific time instants.
- One way to implement a schedular that makes scheduling decisions periodically is to use a H/w timer.
- The timer is set to expire periodically without the intervention of the scheduler.
- When system is initialized, the scheduler selects and schedules the job that will execute until the next scheduling decision time.
- When the timer expires the scheduler awakes and repeats these actions.
- Schedule is stored in a table.
- Schedule invoked by a time.

Weighted Round-Robin Approach: (OR) Processor Sharing Algorithm

- This approach is commonly used for time shared application.
- When jobs are scheduled on a round-robin basis every job joins FIFO Queue and when it ready for execution.
- If the job is not complete by the end of the time slice then the job is placed at the end of the Queue.
- There are n jobs ready for execution, each job gets $Y_{n\text{th}}$ share of the processor time *i.e.*, why called **"processor sharing algorithm"**.
- Weighted round-robin algorithm has been used for scheduling real-time traffic in high speed switched N/ws.
- Weight of the job refers to the fraction of processor time allocated to the job.
- A job with weights wt gets wt time slices every round. The length of a round is equal to the sum of the weights of all the fig. round-robin scheduling of precedence constrained jobs.

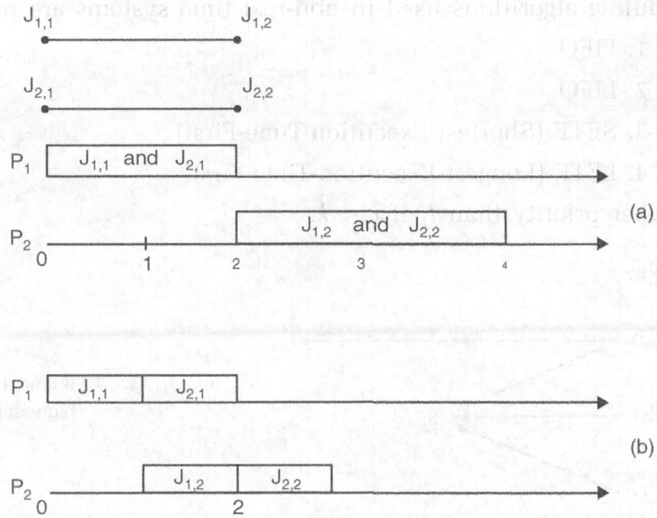

Fig. 2.6

- By adjusting the jobs we can speed up the job process time.

  Example: Consider 2 sets of jobs J_1 and J_2

  J_1 consists of $J_1 = \{J_{1,1}, J_{1,2}\}$

  J_2 consists of $J_2 = \{J_{2,1}, J_{2,2}\}$
- The release times of all jobs are 0, and their executions times a real.
- $J_{1,1}$ and $J_{2,1}$ execute on processor P_1, and $J_{1,2}$ and $J_{2,2}$ execute on processor P_2.

PRIORITY-DRIVEN APPROACH

- Priority driven algorithms are also called "event driven".
- Other commonely used names for this approach are "greedy scheduling", "list scheduling" and "work conserving scheduling".
- Priorities are assigned off-line or on-line.
- Static priority:

  Example: RM (Rate Monotonic), DM (Deadline Monotonic)
- Dynamic priority:

  Example: EDF (Earliest Deadline First) or least time to go.
- It is greedy, because it tries to make locally optional decisions.
- Scheduling decisions are made when the event such is releases and completions of jobs occur.
- Priority driven algorithm can be implemented by assigning priorities to jobs.
- Jobs ready for execution are placed in one or more queues and by the priorities to the jobs.

- Most scheduling algorithms used in non-real time systems are priority driven.

  Example: 1. FIFO
  2. LIFO
  3. SETF (Shortest-Execution-Time-First)
  4. LETF (Longest-Execution-Time-First)
- J_i has a higher priority than J_k if $i < k$.

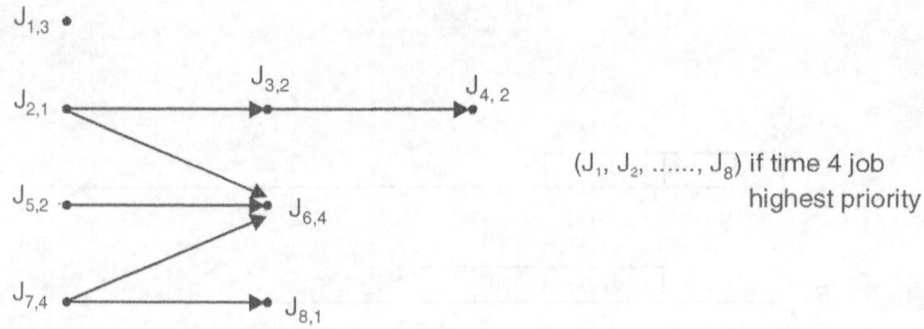

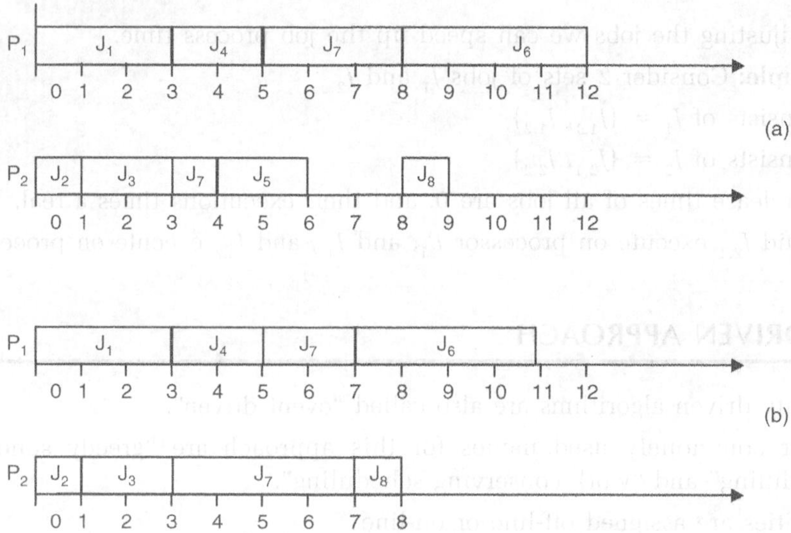

Fig. 2.7. *Example of priority-driven scheduling (a) preemptive (b) Non preemptive.*

Earliest Deadline First (EDF) or Least Time to Go is a dynamic scheduling algorithm used in real-time operating systems. It placs processes in a priority queue. Whenever a scheduling event occurs (task finishes, new task released, etc.) the queue will be searched for the process closest to its deadline. This process is the next to be scheduled for execution.

EDF is an *optional* scheduling algorithm on preemptive uniprocessors, in the following sense: if a collection of independent *jobs*, each characterised by an arrival time, an execution requirement, and a deadline, can be scheduled (by any algorithm) such that all the jobs complete by their deadlines, the **EDF** will schedule this collection of jobs such that they all completes by their deadlines.

With scheduling periodic processes that have deadlines equal to their periods, **EDF** has a utilization bound of 100%. Thus, the schedulability test for **EDF** is:

$$U = \sum_{i=1}^{n} \frac{C_i}{T_i} \leq 1$$

That is, EDF can guarantee that all deadlines are met provided that the total CPU utilization is not more than 100%. So, compared to fixed priority scheduling techniques like rate-monotonic scheduling, **EDF** can guarantee all the deadlines in the system at higher loading.

However, when the system is overloaded, the set of processes that will miss deadlines is largely unpredictable (it will be a function of the exact deadlines and time at which the overload occurs.) This is a considerable disadvantage to a real-time systems designer. The algorithm is also difficult to implement in hardware and there is a tricky issue of representing deadlines in different ranges (deadlines must be rounded to finite amounts, typically a few bytes at most). If one uses modular arithmetic to calculate future deadlines relative to now, the field storing a future relative deadline must accommodate at least the value of the (("duration" {of the longest expected time to completion} * 2) + "now"). Therefore, **EDF** is not commonly found in industrial real-time computer systems.

Instead, most real-time computer systems use fixed priority scheduling (usually rate-monotonic scheduling). With fixed priorities, it is easy to predict that overload conditions will cause the low-priority processes to miss deadlines, while the highest-priority process will still meet its deadline.

There is a significant body of research dealing with **EDF** scheduling in real-time computing; it is possible to calculate worst case response times of processes in **EDF**, to deal with other types of processes than periodic processes and to use servers to regulate overloads.

Example:

Consider 3 periodic processes scheduled using **EDF**, the following acceptance test shows that all deadlines will be met.

Process	**Execution Time = C**	**Period = T**
P1	1	8
P2	2	5
P3	4	10

The utilization will be:

$$\left(\frac{1}{8}\right) + \left(\frac{2}{5}\right) + \left(\frac{4}{10}\right) = 0.925 = 92.5\%$$

The theoretical limit for any number of processes is 100% and so the system is schedulable.

Preemptive

- The running task can be interrupted at any time to assign the processor to anther active task, according to a predefined scheduling policy.

Non-preemptive

- A task, once started, is executed until completion.

Dynamic Versus Static Systems

- When a processor is available, the job at the head of the queue executes on the processor such systems are called *"Dynamic system"*.
- Because jobs are dynamically dispatched to processors.
- Multiprocessor system also called **'Dynamic system'**.
- Each preempted job to resume on any processor.
- Jobs are moved among processors only when the system must be reconfigured.
- When operation mode of the system changes or some processors fail. Such system is called a **"static system"**. Because system is statically configured.

  Example: Divide the total jobs into for 2 processors

  J_1, J_2, J_6, J_7 execute-processor P_1

  J_3, J_5, J_4, J_8 execute-processor P_2

  Such system is called static system.

EFFECTIVE RELEASE TIME AND DEADLINES

- Release time of a job may be later than that of its successors and its deadline may be earlier than that of its predecessors.

Effective Release Time

- The effective Release time of a job without predecessors is equal to its given release time.
- The effective Release time of a job with predecessors is equal to its maximum value among its given release time and the effective release times of all of its predecessors.

Effective Deadline

- The effective deadline of a job without a successor is equal to its given deadline.
- The effective deadline of a job with successors is equal to the minimum value among its given deadlines. The effective deadlines of all of its successors.

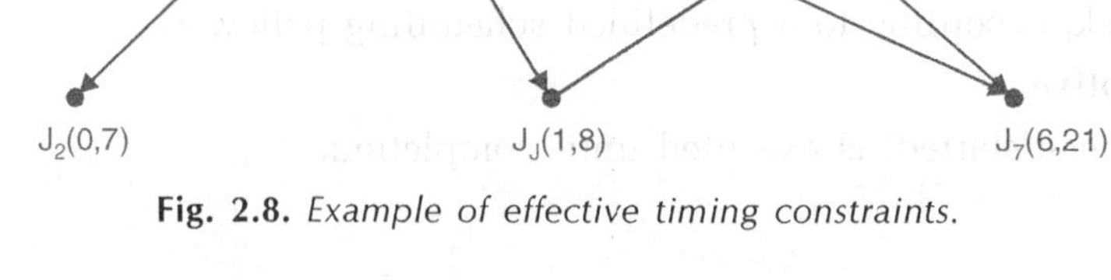

Fig. 2.8. *Example of effective timing constraints.*

$J_1(2, 8)$ $J_5(2, 8)$
$J_2(0, 7)$ $J_6(4, 20)$
$J_3(2, 8)$ $J_7(6, 21)$
$J_4(4, 9)$

Offline Versus Online Scheduling

- The schedule is computed off-line before the system begins to execute the computation is based on the knowledge of Release time and processor time/resource requirement of all jobs for all times. A schedule is generated before actual task activation.
  Disadvantage: Of offline scheduling is inflexibility.
- This offline scheduling is possible only item the system is deterministic meaning that the system provides some fixed set (*s*) of functions and release times.

Online Scheduling

- Scheduling decisions without knowledge about the jobs that will be released in the future.
- The parameters of each job become known to the online scheduler only after the job is released.
- Online scheduling is the only option in a system whose future works is unpredictable.
- Scheduling decisions are taken at runtime every time a new task enters the system or when a running task terminates.

OPTIMAL VERSUS HEURISTIC SCHEDULING

Optimal Scheduling

- An algorithm is said to be optimal if it minimizes some given cost functions defined over the task set.

Heuristic Scheduling

- An algorithm is said to be heuristic if it tends towards but does not guarantee to find the optimal schedule.

❑❑❑

Unit 3 REAL-TIME OPERATING SYSTEM

- **Operating Systems: Overview,**
- Time services and scheduling mechanisms,
- Other basic operating system function,
- Processor reserves and resource kernel.
- Capabilities of commercial real-time operating systems.

OPERATING SYSTEMS

Introduction

Real-Time Operating Systems

"A real-time application requires a program to respond to stimuli within some small upper limit of response time."

A real-time operating system (RTOS) is designed to support real-time applications.

And therefore delivers its services under defined time constraints.

The fundamentals

Real-time and embedded systems operate in constrained environments in which computer memory and processing power are limited. They often need to provide their services within strict time deadlines to their users and to the surrounding world. It is these memory, speed and timing constraints that dictate the uses of real-time operating systems in embedded software.

Basic Kernel Services

We will focus on the "kernel" – the part of an operating system that provides the most basic services to application software running on a processor.

The "kernel" of a real-time operating system ("RTOS") provides an "abstraction layer" that hides from application software the hardware details of the processor (or set of processors) upon which the application software will run. This is shown in Figure 3.1.

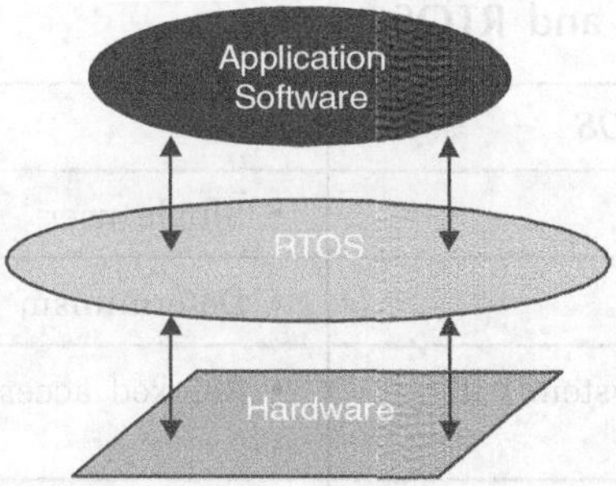

Fig. 3.1. *An RTOS Kernel provides an Abstraction Layer between Application Software and Embedded Hardware.*

In providing this "abstraction layer" the RTOS kernel supplies five main categories of basic services to application software, as seen in Figure 3.2.

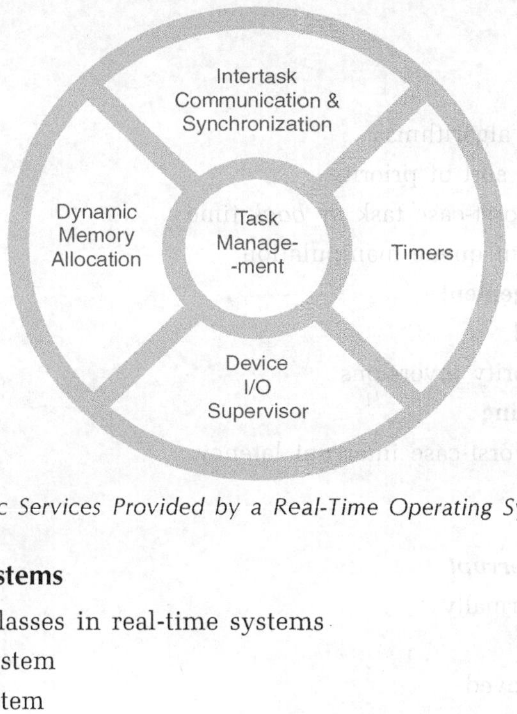

Fig. 3.2. *Basic Services Provided by a Real-Time Operating System Kernel.*

Classes of Real-Time Systems

There are two types of classes in real-time systems

1. Hard real-time system
2. Soft real-time system

Hard Real-time System

- Failure to meet deadlines is fatal.
- Validation by formal methods or extensive simulation.
- Flight control system.

Soft Real-time System

- Late completion of tasks is undesirable but not fatal.
- System performance degrades as more tasks miss deadlines.
- DVD player.

Comparisons between GPOS and RTOS

General-purpose OS	*Real-Time OS*
• Multi-user	• Single user
• Timesharing	• Determinism
• Access control, protection, system call interface, etc	• Relaxed access control and protection (if any)
• Applications	• Applications
• Independently run under the control of the OS	• Tied together with the RTOS

RTOS Typical Features

1. **Scheduling**
    - Deterministic algorithms
    - Usually some sort of priority
    - Predictable worst-case task *fly back* time
    - Concerns about queue manipulation
2. **Resource Management**
    - Low overhead
    - Aware of priority inversions
3. **Interrupt Handling**
    - Guaranteed worst-case interrupt latency.

Handling an Interrupt

Important Points of Interrupt

1. Program runs normally
2. Interrupt occurs
3. Processor state saved
4. Interrupt routine runs
5. "Return from Interrupt" instruction runs
6. Processor state restored
7. Normal program execution resumes.

Interrupt Service Routines

Most interrupt routines do as little as possible:

- Copy peripheral data into a buffer
- Indicate to other code that data has arrived
- Acknowledge the interrupt (tell hardware).

Additional processing usually deferred to outside. *e.g.*, Interrupt causes a process to start or resume running objective: let the OS handle scheduling, not the interrupting peripherals.

Over View

The terms commonly used in O.S. literature. We make several assumptions about the implementation of the application and the architecture of the operating system.

- Threads and Tasks
- Periodic Threads
- Aperiodic, Sporadic and Server Threads

The Kernel

System Call

Time Services and Scheduling

External Interrupts

↓

Interrupt scheduling classified into 2 types

↳ Immediate Interrupt Services

↳ Scheduled Interrupt Services

TIME SERVICES AND SCHEDULING MECHANISMS

Time Services

Clocks and time

Resolution

Hi-Resolution

Timers and Timer functions

Asynchronous Timer functions

Synchronous Timer functions

Timer Resolution

Periodic Timer interrupts

One-shot timer interrupts

Timer Accuracy

Release-time Jitters of periodic Tasks

Scheduling Mechanisms

Fixed-Priority Scheduling

EDF Scheduling

Preemption Lock

Aperiodic-Thread Scheduling

OTHER BASIC O.S. FUNCTIONS

- **Communication and Synchronization**
  Message queues
  Prioritization
  Priority Restoration
  Ceiling-priority Protocol
  Message-Based Priority Inheritance
  No block and Notification
  Synchronization mechanisms
  Basic primitives
  Inheritance function
- **Event Notification and Software Interrupt**
  Signal and similar mechanisms
  More on signals
  R.T. posix signals
  Overhead and timing predictability
- **Memory Management**
  Virtual memory mapping
  Memory locking
  Memory protection
- **I/O and Networking**
  Multi Thread-Architecture
  Early Demultiplexing
  Light weight protocol stack

CAPABILITIES OF COMMERCIAL RTOS's

- Comformance to standards
- Modularity and scalability
- Speed and Efficiency
- System calls
- Split Interrupt handling
- Scheduling
- Priority Inversion Control
- Clock and Timer Resolution
- Memory management

Commercial RTOS Examples and Features and Their Comparisons

- Lynx OS
- QNX/Neutrino

- VRTx
- Vx works
- Spring kernel
- PSO system

Open Source RTOS Examples

- eCos
- Free RTOS
- RT Linux
- RTAI
- Micro C/osII

OTHER BASIC O.S. FUNCTIONS

An O.S. services that are essential for all but the simplest embedded applications.

Real-time issues in

↳ Communication and synchronization

↳ s/w interrupt (software interrupt)

↳ mem. management (memory management)

↳ I/o (Input/Output)

↳ N/wing (Networking).

Communication and Synchronization

As they execute, threads communicate (*i.e.,* they exchange control infor. and data). They synchronize in order to ensure that their exchanges occur at the right times and under the right conditions and that they do not get into each other's way. **Shared mem, message queues, synchronization primitives** (*e.g.,* mutexes, condition variables and semaphores) and **events** and **signals** are commonly used mechanisms for these purposes. Shared members provide a low-level, Hi-B.W. and low-latency means of IPC.

Message Queues

A message queue provides a place, where one or more threads can pass messages to some other thread or threads. Message Queues provide a file-like interface. They are an easy-to-use means of many-to-many communication among threads.

Real-time POSIX message Queue interface functions, such as

↳ mq-Send( )

↳ mq-Receive( ),

can be implemented as fast and efficient library functions.

clients, SSP (sys. service provider)

server, RFS (request-for-service)

Prioritization

Messages in Real-time POSIX message queues have priorities in the range [0, MAX_PR]

| ms_send( ) |

[O, MQ_MAX_PRIO]

where, the number MQ_MAX_PRIO of message priorities is at least 31.

General O.S. supports two priorities → normal

levels → urgent

MESSAGE BASED PRIORITY INHERITANCE

No Block and Notification

A useful feature is nonblocking. The Real-time POSIX message queue send function **mq_send( )** is nonblocking. **O_NONBLOCK** a thread is blocked if the message queue is empty when it calls mq_receive( ). We can make receive call nonblocking in the same manner.

Notification means that a message queue notifies a process when the queue changes from being **empty to non-empty.**

Synchronization Mechanism

Fixed priority ceiling protocol uses this mechanism

CPP (ceiling-priority protocol), is sometimes called a "poor man's priority ceiling-protocol".

Basic primitives: Here that the O.S. provides two functions

inherit_pr( )

restore_pr( )

A resource manager within the O.S. or at the user level can use them to raise and restore the priorities of threads,

- The function inherit_pr(TH) is called when a thread is defined a resource *R* and becomes blocked.
- The function restore_pr( ) is called when a resource is released. It has two parameters:

  The name of the resource that has just been released

  The ID of the thread which releases the resources.

Inheritance function:

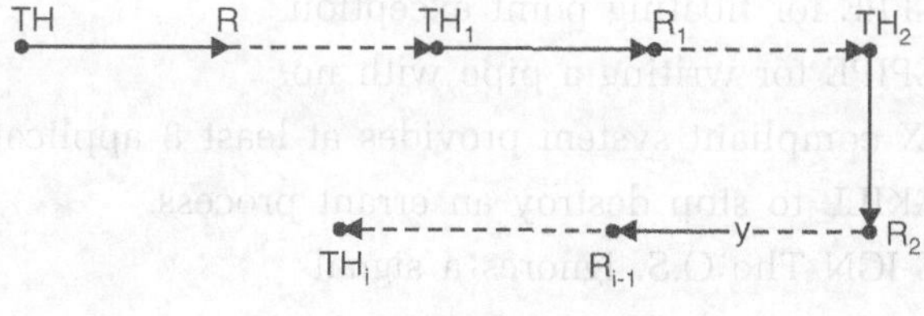

Blocking chain

Priority Restoration

A thread may hold multiple resources at the same time and may inherit different priorities as others threads becomes blocked when they contend for these resources.

TCB-Thread central block that holds information restore_pr( )_inherit_pr( ) for each thread in it **TCB** as a linked list of records. The list is called on **Inheritance log (IL).**

restore_pr(TH, R)

restore_pr( ) does not change its priority,

restore_pr( ) computes the new thread priority called 'π_r'

Ceiling-Priority Protocol

The resource manager generates from this knowledge the priority ceiling π (*R*) of every resource *R*.

EVENT NOTIFICATION AND S/W INTERRUPT

Event Notification, exception handling and s/w interrupts are essential for multitasking systems.

Signal and Similar Mechanisms

In UNIX system, interrupt handlers and the kernel use signals as a means to inform threads of the occurrences of exceptions. (**Ex.:** divide by zero and bad system call) or waited for events. A thread may signal another thread to synchronize and communicate. When the kernel delivers a signal to the thread, the signal handler executes. Thus, the signal mechanism provides synchrony and immediacy, just as H/w interrupt do.

NON-UNIX system typically provide these capabilities using more than one mechanism. As **Ex.:** in windows NT, events and Asynchronous Procedure Calls (APCs) serve the same purpose as signals in UNIX system.

The PSO system [Moto] provides events and asynchronous signals. The formers are synchronous and point to point. An event is sent to a specified Receiving task.

More on Signals

Internal to UNIX O.S. signals used for different purposes are identified by numbers.

The header file < signal.h >; most POSIX signals are used by the O.S.:

SIGALRM for signaling upon timer expiration

SIGTERM for terminating a process

SIGFPE for floating point exception

SIGPIPE for writing a pipe with no.

A Real-time POSIX compliant system provides at least 8 application-defined signals.

SIGKILL to stop destroy an errant process

SIG-IGN The O.S. ignores a signal

Sigaction( )

a mask SA-mask and a flag field SA-flag. A process (thread) can ask the O.S. to set these members by calling **sigaction( )**.

R.T. POSIX Signals

There are at least 8 Application-defined R.T. signals versus only **two** provided by POSIX. These signals are numbered from SIGRTMIN to SIGRTMAX

5th POSIX R.T. extensions provides a new and more responsive synchronous signal-wait function called "Sigwait info."

5th number signal

2nd number signal

3rd number signal

4th number signal

2nd → real-time signals can be queued

3rd → a Q.R.T. signal can carry data

4th → Queued signals are prioritized

MEMORY MANAGEMENT

They are ↳ virtual memory mapping ↳ memory locking

↳ paging

↳ memory protection.

All general purpose O.S. support virtual memory and memory protection not all R.T.O.S. do and those that to typically provide the user with the choice of protection or no protection.

VIRTUAL MEMORY MAPPING

We can divide R.T.O.S. into **three** categories depending on whether they support virtual memory mapping and paging (*i.e.*, demand paging or swapping). R.T.O.S primarily for E.R.T. applications such as **data acquisition. Signal processing and monitoring** may not support virtual memory mapping. **The PSoSystem is an example.**

Upon request, the system creates physically contiguous blocks of memory for the applications. The application may request variable size segments from its memory block and define a memory partition consisting of physically contiguous, fixed size buffers.

Memory fragmentation is a potential problem for a system that does not support virtual mapping.

The penalty of virtual address mapping is the address translation table which must be maintained and hence contribute to the size of the O.S. Moreover, it complicates DMA controlled I/O.

MEMORY LOCKING

A R.T.O.S. may support paging so that non realtime, memory demanding Applications (Ex: editors, debuggers and performance profilers) needed during development can run together with target real-time applications. Such an O.S. must provide applications with some means to control paging.

Ex.: R.T. POSIX-Compliant system allow an application to pin down in memory all of its pages [*i.e.,* mlockall( )] or a range of pages *i.e.,* mlock( ) with the starting address of the address range and the length of the range as parameters.

– The Lynxos O.S. control paging according to the **demand-paging priority.**

MEMORY PROTECTION

Many R.T.O.S. **Ex.:** QNX and LynxOS support memory protection.

A good alternative is to provide the application with the choices in memory management such as the choices in virtual memory configuration offered by **Vx works [wind]** and QNX. In Vxworks, we can choose (configuration in configAll.h) to have only virtual address mapping, to have text segments and exception, vectors tables write protected.

I/O AND NETWORKING

Three modern features of file system and networking software are

↳ multithreaded-server architecture

↳ early demultiplexing

↳ lightweight protocol stock

These features were developed to improve the performance of time-shared applications Hi-performance applications and N/w appliances.

MULTITHREADED SERVER ARCHITECTURE

Servers in modern O.S. are typically multithreaded. In response to request, such a server activates (creates) a work thread to service the request.

If the server were single-threaded, a client might be blocked for the entire duration when the server executes on behalf of another client and the blocking time can be order of magnitude larger. We can model the client thread as an end-to-end Job consisting of a CPU subjob, which is followed by a disk access sub Job and the disk-access Job executes on the disk system and is in turn followed by a CPU subjob. Both CPU subjobs have the same priority as the client thread.

EARLY DEMULTIPLEXING

Traditional protocol handlers are based on layered architectures. They can introduce **a large blocking time.**

Ex.: When packets arrive over a TCP/IP connection, the protocol module in the N/W layer ACK's the receipts of the packets, strips away their headers, reassembles them into IP datagrams and hands off the datagram to the IP module after each datagram is reassembled. The protocol modules executes at a higher priority than all user threads and blocks Hi-priority threads when they process packets of low-priority clients.

Early demultiplexing also makes it possible to eliminate the extra copying. Some communication mechanisms **Ex.:** Illinios FM (Fost Massage] [PaLC] for Hi-speed local N/W take this approach. The fact that messages are copied directly b/w the N/W interface card and the application is a major reason that these mechanisms can achieve an end-to-end (application-application) latency in order of 10 to 20 μsec.

LIGHT WEIGHT PROTOCOL STACK

Protocol processing can introduce large overhead and long latency. This is especially true when the protocol stack has the client/server structure: each Higher-level protocol modules uses the services provided by a protocol module at a layer below.

A challenge is how to provide lightweight, low overhead protocol processing and still retain the adv. of the layer architecture.

An **Ex.:** of O.S designed to meet this challenge is the **Scout O.S.** MMOP, MOPe. Scout is based on the path abstraction. Scout uses paths as a means to speed up the data delivery between the N/W and applications.

COMMERCIAL REAL-TIME OPERATING SYSTEMS – AN INTRODUCTION

- Introduction
- LynxOS
- QNX/Neutrino
- VRTX

- VxWorks
- Spring Kernel
- pSOSystem

Introduction

A real-time operating system (RTOS) [Generally pronounced as: Are-toss] is a multitasking operating system intended for real-time applications. Such applications include embedded systems (programmable thermostats, household appliance controllers, mobile telephones), industrial robots, spacecraft, industrial control (see SCADA), and scientific research equipment.

An RTOS facilitates the creation of a real-time system, but does not guarantee the final result will be real-time; this requires correct development of the software. An RTOS does not necessarily have high throughput; rather, an RTOS provides facilities which, if used properly, guarantee deadlines can be met generally (soft real-time) or deterministically (hard real-time). An RTOS will typically use specialized scheduling algorithms in order to provide the real-time developer with the tools necessary to produce deterministic behaviour in the final system. An RTOS is valued more for how quickly and/or predictably it can respond to a particular event than for the given amount of work it can perform over time. Key factors in an RTOS are therefore a minimal interrupt latency and a minimal thread switching latency.

- Commercial RTOSs different from traditional OS – gives more predictability
- Used in the following areas such as:
  - Embedded Systems or Industrial Control Systems.
  - Parallel and Distributed Systems.
- *E.g.*, LynxOS, VxWorks, pSoS, QNX, bluecat.
- Traditionally, these systems can be classified into a Uniprocessor, Multiprocessor or Distributed Real-Time OS.

Lynx OS

Introduction

- Microkernel design
  1. Means the kernel footprint is small
  2. Only 28 KB in size
- The small kernel provides essential services in scheduling, interrupt dispatching and synchronization.
- The other services are provided by kernel lightweight service modules, called Kernel Plug-Ins (KPIs).
- New KPIs can be added to the microkernel and can be configured to support I/O, file systems, TCP/IP, streams and sockets.
- Can function as a multipurpose UNIX OS.
- Here, KPIs are multi-threaded, which means each KPI can create as many threads as it want.

- There is no context switch when sending a message to a KPI.
  - For example, when a RFS (Request for Service) message is sent to a File System KPI, this does not request a context switch.
  - Hence, run-time overhead is minimum.
  - Further, inter KPI communication incurs minimal overhead with it consuming only very few instructions.
- **Lynx OS** is a self hosted system—wherein development can be done in the same system.
- In such a system, there is a need for protecting the OS from such huge memory consuming applications (compilers, debuggers).
- Lynx OS offers memory protection through hardware MMUs.
- Applications make I/O requests to I/O system through system calls.
- Kernel directs I/O request to the device driver.
- Each device driver has an interrupt handler and kernel thread.
- The interrupt handler carries the first step of interrupt handling.
- If it does not complete the processing, it sets an asynchronous trap to the kernel.
- Later, when kernel can respond to the software interrupt, it schedules an instance of the kernel thread to complete the interrupt processing.

QNX/Neutrino

Introduction

- POSIX-compliant Unix-like real-time operating system.
- Microkernel design–kernel provides essential threads and real-time services.
- Use of a microkernel allows users (developers) to turn off any functionality they do not require without having to change the OS itself.
- The system is quite small, fitting in a minimal fashion on a single floppy, and is considered to be both very fast and fairly "complete."
- The footprint of microkernel is 12kb.
- Every driver, application, protocol stack, and file system runs outside the kernel, in the safety of memory-protected user space.
- As a result, virtually any component can fail—and be automatically restarted -without affecting other components or the kernel.
- Maximize application portability with extensive support for the POSIX standard, which lets you quickly migrate Linux, Unix, and other open source programs.
- QNX is a message passing operating system.
  - Messages are basic means of interprocess communication among all threads.
  - Follows a message based priority tracking feature.

VRTX (Virtual Real-Time Executive)

Introduction

- VRTX has **two** multitasking kernels
  - **VRTXsa (scalable architecture)**
    - ★ Designed for performance
    - ★ Provides priority inheritance, POSIX compliant libraries
    - ★ Supports multiprocessing
    - ★ System calls fully preemptable and deterministic
  - **VRTXmc (micro-controller)**
    - ★ Designed for low memory consumption
    - ★ Used for cellular phones and hand-held devices
    - ★ Rather than providing optional components provides hooks for extensibility – application can add its own system calls

VxWorks

Introduction

- Created by Wind River.
- Current Version: VxWorks 6.0 →
- VxWorks is the most established and most widely deployed device software operating system.
- Currently there are more than 300 million devices that are VxWorks enabled.
- The core attributes of VxWorks, include high performance, reliability, determinism, low latency and scalability.
- Enhanced error management.
- Backward compatibility to previous version features for exception handling and template support.
- Extensive POSIX 1003.1, .1b, .1c compatibility (including pthreads).
- Scheduling
  - Uses preemptive priority with round robin scheduling to accommodate for both
    - ★ Real-time processes
    - ★ Non-real time processes
- Memory Protection
  - MMU based memory protection.
- Reduced Context Switch time
  - Saves only those register windows that are actually in use (on a Sparc)
  - When a task's context is restored, only the relevant register window is restored

  - To increase response time, it saves the register windows in a register cache – useful for recurring tasks
- **Distinguishing features**
  - efficient POSIX-compliant memory management
  - multiprocessor facilities
  - shell for user interface
  - symbolic and source level debugging capabilities
  - performance monitoring
- Mars Exploration Rovers *Spirit* and *Opportunity* and the Mars Reconnaissance Orbiter use the VxWorks operating system.

pSOSystem

Introduction

pSOSystem is a modular, high-performance real-time operating system designed specifically for embedded microprocessors. It provides a complete multitasking environment based on open systems standards.

pSOSystem is designed to meet three overriding objectives:

- Performance
- Reliability
- Ease-of-Use

The result is a fast, deterministic, yet accessible system software solution. Accessible in this case translates to a minimal learning curve. pSOSystem is designed for quick startup on both custom and commercial hardware. The pSOSystem software is supported by an integrated set of cross development tools that can reside on UNIX- or DOS-based computers. These tools can communicate with a target over a serial or TCP/IP network connection.

The pSOSystem software employs a modular architecture. It is built around the pSOS+ real-time multi-tasking kernel and a collection of companion software components. Software components are standard building blocks delivered as absolute position-independent code modules.

In addition to these core components, pSOSystem includes the following:

- Networking protocols including SNMP, FTP, Telnet, TFTP, NFS, and STREAMS
- Run-time loader
- User application shell
- Support for C++ applications
- Boot ROMs
- Pre-configured versions of pSOSystem for popular commercial hardware
- pSOSystem templates for custom configurations
- Chip-level device drivers
- Sample applications

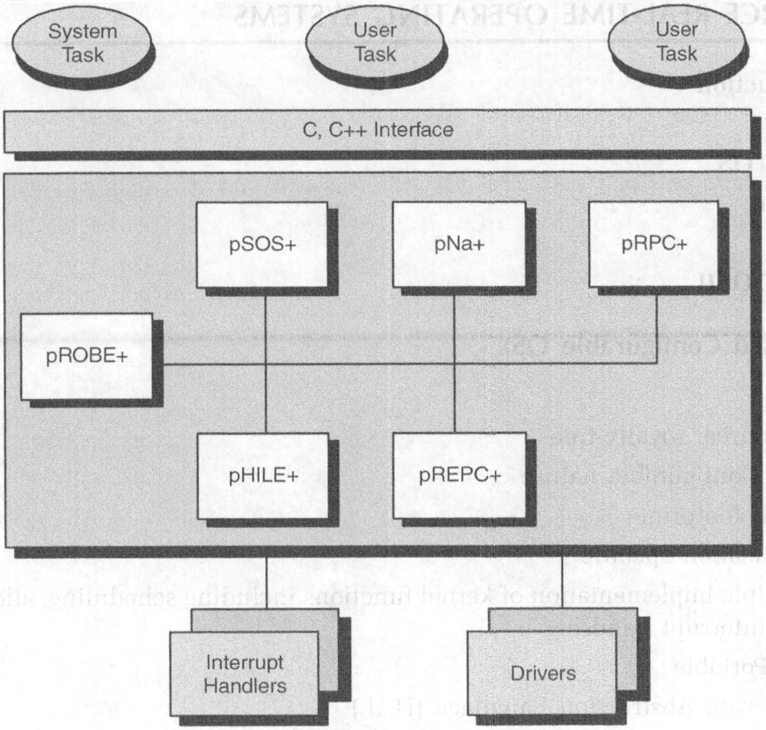

Fig. 3.3. *The pSOSystem Environment.*

The pSOSystem components are listed below.

- **pSOS+ Real-time Multitasking Kernel.** A field-proven, multitasking kernel that provides a responsive, efficient mechanism for coordinating the activities of your real-time system.
- **pSOS+m Multiprocessor Multitasking Kernel**. Extends the pSOS+ feature set to operate seamlessly across multiple, tightly-coupled or distributed processors.
- **pNA+ TCP/IP Network Manager.** A complete TCP/IP implementation including gateway routing, UDP, ARP, and ICMP protocols; uses a standard socket interface that includes stream, datagram, and raw sockets.
- **pRPC+ Remote Procedure Call Library.** Offers SUN-compatible RPC and XDR services; allows you to build distributed applications using the familiar C procedure paradigm.
- **pHILE+ File System Manager**. Gives efficient access to mass storage devices, both local and on a network. Includes support for CD-ROM devices, MS-DOS compatible floppy disks, and a high-speed proprietary file system. When used in conjunction with the pNA+ component and the pRPC+ subcomponent, offers client- side NFS services.
- **pREPC+ ANSI C Standard Library**. Provides familiar ANSI C run-time functions such as printf( ), scanf( ), and so forth, in the target environment. The above Figure illustrates the pSOSystem environment.

OPEN SOURCE REAL-TIME OPERATING SYSTEMS

- **Introduction**
- **eCos**
- **Free RTOS**
- **RTLinux**
- **RTAI**
- **MicroC/OSII**

eCos (Embedded Configurable OS)

Introduction

- open source, royalty-free
- Highly Configurable nature
  - Small footprint
  - Application specific
  - Multiple implementation of kernel functions including scheduling, allocating memory and interrupt handling
- Easily Portable
  - Hardware Abstraction Language (HAL)
  - Native API, POSIX API, μITRON API, C API
- eCos is targeted at high-volume applications in consumer electronics, telecommunications, automotive, and other deeply embedded applications.
- eCos has kernel mode
  - No user mode
- Implemented using C++
- GNU debugger (GDB) support.

Features

- Choice of scheduling algorithms
- Choice of memory-allocation strategies
- Timers and counters
- Support for interrupts and DSRs
- Exception handling
- ISO C library, Math library
- Rich set of synchronization primitives
- Host debug and communications support.

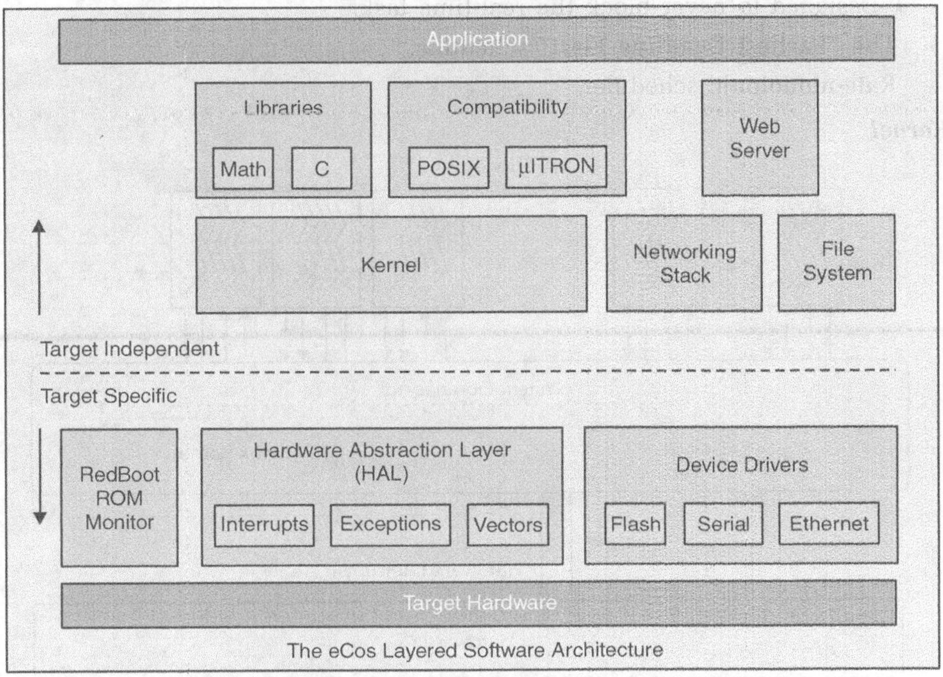

Fig. 3.4. *The eCos Layered Software Architecture abstracts target details from the high-level application, providing excellent platform portability, while still maintaining performance at the low-level target drivers and services.*

RTLinux

Introduction

- Available as a patch to the regular Linux kernel.
- Provides an RT API for developers.
- RTLinux is a hybrid OS that runs a Linux kernel as an idle thread (lowest priority) of the real-time kernel.
- Predictable delays.
  - By its small size and limited operations.
- Finer timer resolution.
- RT kernel and RT applications are kept as simple as possible and non-time critical applications (GUIs, file systems) are handled by the standard Linux.
- Real-time threads and interrupt handlers never delayed by non-realtime operations.
- Preemptible kernel.
  - Its routines are very small and fast, this does not cause big delays.
  - Interrupts from Linux are disabled.
- RT-Linux has many kinds of Schedulers.
  - **FIFO.**
    - ⋆ Used to pass information between real-time process and ordinary Linux process.

★ Designed to never block the real-time task.

– The "**Earliest Deadline First**" scheduler.

– **Rate-monotonic** scheduler.

Linux Kernel

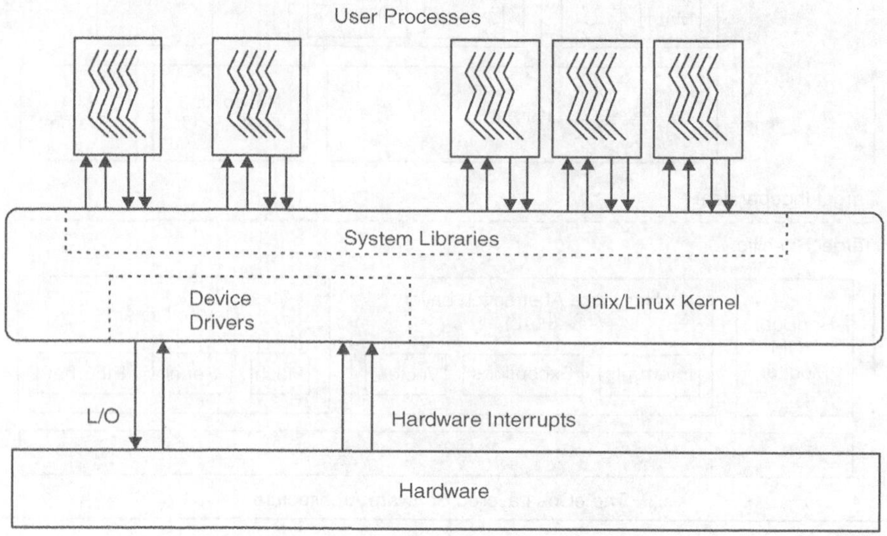

Fig. 3.5. *Detail of the bare linux kernel.*

RTLinux Kernel

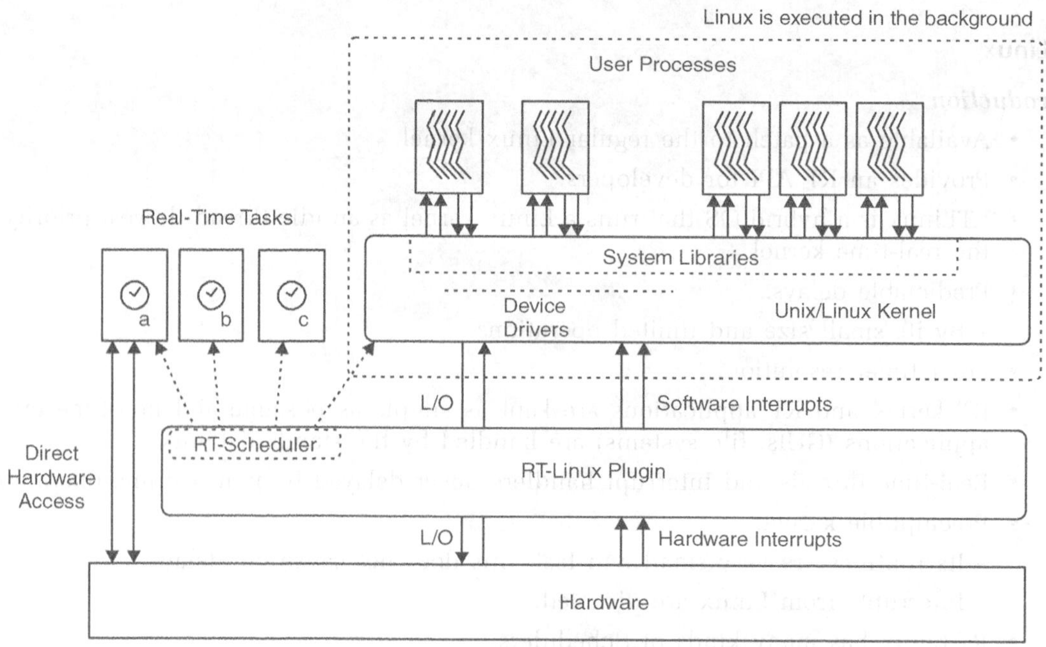

Fig. 3.6. *Detail of the RTLinux kernel.*

RTAI (Real Time Application Interface)

Introduction

- Hard real-time extension to the Linux kernel.
- A patch to the Linux kernel which introduces a hardware abstraction layer.
- A broad variety of services which make real-time programmers' life's easier.
- RTAI provides deterministic response to interrupts, POSIX compliant and native RTAI real-time tasks.
- Linux application is able to execute without any modification.
- RTAI considers Linux as a background task running when no real time activity occurs.
- RTAI is very much module oriented.
- Real time scheduler module.
  - Task functions.
  - Timing functions.
  - Semaphore functions.
  - Mailbox functions.
  - Intertask communication functions.
- FIFO services.
- Shared memory.
- POSIX pthread and pqueue (msg queue).

Comparison of Linux implementations RTLinux and RTAI

- RTAI provides better real-time support than RTLinux
  - soft real-time in user space along with hard real-time in kernel space.
  - excellent performance in terms of low jitter and low latency.
  - better C++ support and more complete feature set.

MicroC/OSII

Introduction

- Also known as μC/OS II or uC/OSII.
- MicroC/OS has been designed as a small footprint real time pre-emptive OS that was designed for embedded use on 8 bit platforms upwards.
- Highly portable, ROMable, very scalable, preemptive real-time, multitasking kernel.
- Has ports for most popular processors and boards in the market.
- Suitable for use in safety critical embedded systems such as aviation, medical systems and nuclear installations.
- Over 100 microprocessors are supported.
- Approved for use in a DO-178B aerospace system and is (apparently) MISRA-C compliant
- **μC/OS II features**
  - reentrant functions and is portable to different processors

- kernel is preemptive real time, managing up to 64 tasks, with up to 56 tasks for each application.
- Each task has a unique priority and its own stack.
- Round robin scheduling is not supported.
- operating system uses semaphores to restrict access to resources shared by multiple elements of the system.
- Memory management is performed using fixed size partitions.
- μC/OS-II is a multitasking operating system.
- Each task is an infinite loop and can be in any one of the following 5 states.
- Dormant, Ready, Running, Waiting, ISR.
- services such as mailboxes, queues, and semaphores.

OTHER RTOS

- **Opensource**
  * Nut/OS
  * TRON Project
- **Commercial**
  * BeOS
  * ChorusOS
  * MicroC/OS-II
  * OS-9
  * OSEKtime
  * pSOS
  * μnOS
  * RMX
  * RSX-11
  * RT-11
  * RTOS-UH
  * VRTX

COMPARISON OF RTOS

	VXWorks	pSOS	eCos
Scheduler	Preemptive	Preemptive	Preemptive
Synchronization mechanism	No condition variable	Yes	Yes
POSIX support	Yes	Yes	Linux
Scalable	Yes	Yes	Yes
Custom hw support	BSP	BSP	HAL, I/O package
Kernel size	–	16KB	–
Multiprocessor support	VxMP/ VxFusion (accessories)	PSOS+m kernel	Yes/only basic support (SMP)

COMMERCIAL RTOS BENEFITS

Now, let's talk about doing it right. What does a commercial RTOS offer, that makes business sense?

No wasted time deciding what to do, doing it, etc.

The RTOS is already done. Just learn it and get on with the project!

Thorough documentation

Most commercial RTOSs come with a User's Guide, a Reference Manual, and well-documented code. Not only that, these are accurate and up to date. Most RTOS vendors also offer training.

Proven code

A commercial RTOS is not only debugged, it is *proven*. It has been used by hundreds of users in a multiplicity of ways. Moreover, it continues to be used and tested and latent bugs continue to be found and fixed. A tough RTOS bug can take weeks to find and fix.

Board support and tool integration

A good RTOS comes with a BSP and integration with a good tool suite. These, alone, are often worth the cost, in programming time, of the RTOS. (BSP means "Board Support Package". It includes startup code and device drivers for most on-chip peripherals as well as for a specific development board.)

Well-structured result

The most important benefit of using a commercial RTOS is the resulting well-structured application code. A commercial RTOS requires a programmer to implement his application in the form of pre-defined objects such as tasks, messages, semaphores, etc. There are firm rules for creating and using these objects. A good RTOS detects misuse and informs the programmer immediately, thus saving days of debug time. Equally important, the code ends up with a structure that makes it easier to understand and change in the future – even by a different programmer. The lack of this capability by the typical non-RTOS based spagetti code is a major problem faced by many companies, and it limits their ability to compete successfully.

Universality

Most commercial RTOSs do standard things in standard ways. The result is greater compatibility with other embedded software products. Good commercial RTOSs offer a wide selection of already integrated products such as file managers, networking stacks, graphical user interfaces, etc. You may need one of these in the future. The inability to easily plug one in hurts competitiveness.

CAPABILITIES OF COMMERCIAL RTOS

1. Conformance to standards
2. Modularity and scalability
3. Speed and efficiency
4. System calls
5. Split interrupt handling

6. Scheduling
7. Priority inversion control
8. Clock and timer Resolution
9. Memory management

System calls: The Non-preemptable portions of kernel functions necessary for mutual exclusion are highly optimized and made as short and deterministic as possible.

Split interrupt handling: The non-preemtable portion of interrupt handling and the execution times of immediate interrupt handling routines are kept small. The bulk of the work done to handle each is scheduled and executed at an appropriate priority.

Modularity and scalabity: The kernel is small, and the operating system configurable. The operating system can be scaled down to fit with the application in ROM in small embedded systems. By adding optional components to the kernel, the operating system can be configured to provide I/O file, and networking services.

Speed and effiency: Most of these operating systems are microkernel systems. The microkernel systems have low overhead. This system having very low interrupt latency one to few microseconds.

Networking: The operating systems can be configured to support TCP/IP, streams and so on.

Memory management: The operating system may provide virtual to physical address mapping but does not do paging. The operating systems may not offer memory protection.

Priority Inversion control: The operating system provides priority inheritance but may allow you to disable it to save the overhead of this mechanism if you choose to use a resource access control scheme that does not need priority inheritance the system may also provide ceiling- priority protocol.

Clock and timer resolution: The operating system may provide a nominal timer resolution down to nanoseconds. Even on the fastest processor today, the operating system takes about a microsecond to process a timer interrupt.

❑❑❑

Unit **4** **FAULT TOLERANCE**

- Fault Tolerance Techniques: Introduction
- Fault Causes
- Types
- Detection
- Fault and Error Containment
- Redundancy: Hardware, Software, Time
- Integrated Failure Handling

FAULT TOLERANCE TECHNIQUES

Introduction

The failure rates of real-time computers must be extraordinarily small. Indeed, they must be smaller than the failure rates of the components from which they are builts. Such computers must therefore be **"fault-tolerant"**, *i.e.,* be able to continue operating despite the failure of a limited subset of their hardwares or softwares. They must also be gracefully degradable *i.e.,* as the size of the faulty set increases the system must not suddenly collapse, but continue executing part of its work load, figure shows how a properly designed fault-tolerant system behaves as the failures increase in no scope.

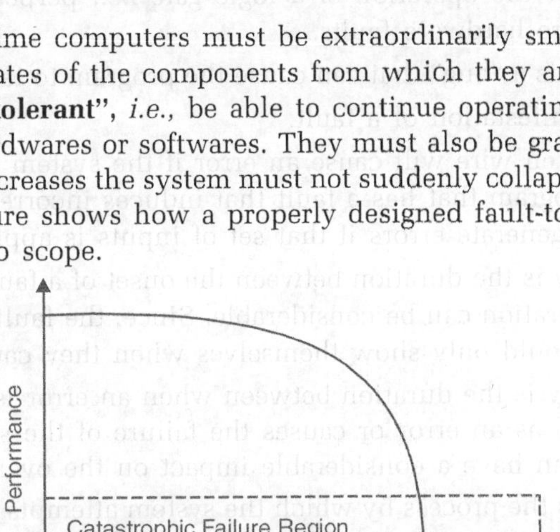

Fig. 4.1

The goal of the system designer is to ensure that the probability of system failure is acceptably small.

- The first step in making a system robust is to reduce the number of faults that the system will encounter. This means decreasing the number of design and manufacturing faults and reducing its vulnerability to disturbances in the operating environment.
- Reducing the incidence of design faults requires careful specification and design, followed by extensive design reviews. The system must be built of High-grade components to reduce the probability of manufacturing defects.

  Example: Each VLSI chip from which it is built must be tested carefully to reduce the probability of using a bad component. Extensive system wide testing must also be conducted before the system is released for use. Indeed, the system must be **designed for testability** *i.e.*, it should be designed to facilitate through testing.
- Making the system robust against interference from the operating environment requires shielding and the use of appropriate (radiation hardened) components.
- But, no matter how robustly the system is designed, it is likely that there will always be faults in it either at the time it is released or later while it is in use. The system must thus be able to tolerate a certain number of failures and still function.
- Since, real-time systems must meet deadlines, there must be both a short-term and a long-term response to failure. The short-term response consists of quickly correcting for a failure to allow immediate deadlines to be met. The long-term response consists of locating the failure, determining the best response to it and initaiting a recovery and reconfiguration procedure.

Definitions

- A **Hardware fault** is some physical defects that can cause a component to malfunction. A broken wire or the operation of a logic gate *i.e.*, perpetually stuck at some logic values (0 or 1) are hardware faults.
- A **software fault** is a "bug" that can cause the program to fail for a given set of inputs.
- A **error** is a manifestation of a fault.

  Example: A broken wire will cause an error if the system tries to propagate a signal through it. A program that has a fault that induces incorrect operations for some set I of inputs will generate errors if that set of inputs is applied.
- The **fault latency** is the duration between the onset of a fault and its manifestation as an error. This duration can be considerable. Since, the faults themselves are invisible to the outside would only show themselves when they cause errors.
- **The error latency** is the duration between when an error is produced and when it is either recognized as an error or causes the failure of the system like fault latencies, error latencies can have a considerable impact on the overall system realiability.
- **Error recovery** is the process by which the system attempts to recover from the effects of an error. There are two forms of error recovery:
  - ★ Forward error recovery
  - ★ Backward error recovery

- **In forward error recovery.** The error is masked without any computations having to be redone.
- **In back error recovery.** The error is masked computations having to be redone. The system is rolled back to a moment in time before the error is believed to have occurred (this roll back involves the restoration of system, state to the state at that moment and the computation is carried out again. This uses **time redundancy.** Since, it consumes additional time to mask the effects of failure.

GENERAL REASONS FOR FAILURES

All projects, whether or not associated with system implementations, can fail for many reasons and rarely is there one specific cause of failure.

The failures of system/ projects are often blamed on 'the way it was implemented', but system implementations can fail as a result of mistakes made before, during or after the Implementation phase of the systems **lifecycle.**

Two characteristics often contribute to the risk of implementation projects.

1. Firstly, they are often attempted by institutions after a long period of stability, implying that there is little organizational experience.
2. Secondly, they vary widely in nature as technology evolves and systems embrace more functionality. Rapid changes in the personal use of technology mean we are often struggling to keep up with the expectations of our learners.

Reviews and assessments of both project successes and **failures** have highlighted that the most salient and momentous parts of any project to be:

- project definition and ultimate objectives;
- specification of software and hardware requirements;
- expectations of the various stakeholders;
- functionality to be provided by the software;
- the contract and on-going relationship with the supplier;
- project plans and progress made within the time scales for each phase;
- the formation and make-up of the steering group and the project teams;
- precise activities carried out by the steering group and the project teams;
- precise software or hardware problems that were reported and the extent to or speed at which they were resolved.

Nevertheless, one thing that stands out in the analysis of systems projects is that few fail for technical reasons. Projects are undoubtedly about people. Most projects fail, because they are not effectively managed and communicated. In those projects, it is almost certain that individuals or groups could and should have reacted differently and taken courses of action that would have given the project a firmer base and/or arrested a decline that continued to gain momentum. Nevertheless, the demoralizing situation in which organizations often find themselves is unlikely to have been because of the culpability of any one individual or third-party.

FAULT/FAILURE CAUSES

There are some causes of failure:

- Errors in the specification or design
- Defects in the components
- Environmental effects
- Poor user interface
- User error
- Hardware error
- Faulty hardware

Errors in the Specifcation or Design

- Mistakes in the specification and design are very difficult to guard against. Many hardware failures and all software failures occur due to such mistakes.
- Specification can be regarded as a mapping from the real world into an artificial specification space. The real world requirements are expressed in formal or informal terms that can be understood by the computer designer.
- The person who writes the specification must thoroughly understand the application and the environment in which that application will operate. The specification is, strictly speaking, the only link in the design process between the real world of the application and the more cloistered world of the computer designer. If the specifications is wrong everything that proceeds from it the design and implementation is likely to be unsatisfactory.
- It is very difficult to ensure that the specification is complelely right. Common sense checks can be made. Specifications can be reviewed by persons unconnected with writing them to increase the chances of mistakes being caught.
- By contrast, the design *i.e.,* developed from a formal specification can theoretically be checked formally. Indeed, any design is just one realization of the specification and theoretically speaking can therefore be formally checked against it.

Defects in the Components

The second cause of faults are defects in components. Hardware components can develop defects. These may arise from manufacturing defects, or from defects caused by the wear and tear of use.

Example: A MOSFET may fail due to electromigration which is the drifting away over time of metal atoms towards the cathode.

Environmental Effects

The third cause of faults are the operating environment. Devices can be subjected to a whole array of stresses, depending on the application. Poor ventilation or excessively High-ambient temperature can melt components or otherwise damage them. If the computer is in a missile, it can undergo High-gravitational-forces and vibrational stress.

Sometimes, especially in aerospace or robotics applications. There can be considerable electromagnetic or elementary particle (such as - α particle) radiation, which can cause spurious changes in the state of F/Fs.

A rough idea of how the reliability of a component can be affected by some of these factors can be obtained by considering the following expression for failure rate, which was developed by the U.S. DOD

$$\lambda = \pi_l \, \pi_Q \, (C_1 \, \pi_J \, \pi_V + C_2 \, \pi_E)$$

π_l : Represents the fabrication process (1 if mature technology ; 10 otherwise).

π_Q : Represents the testing process discord devices that have manufacture (defects range 0.25 and 20).

C_1, C_2 : Complexity factors expressed as a function-of-the number of transistors in the device and the number of pins.

π_T : The effects of temperature and is a function of the type of device (range between 0.1 and 1000).

π_V : Represents the voltage stress on CMOS devices (range 1 to 10).

π_E : Represents other stresses in the operating environment.

Poor User Interface

A poor user interface may cause significant problems for users of the system and thus greatly increase the likelihood of those users introducing to the system data for example that causes system failure. In accounting software for example a single mistake due to poor user interface may cause an invoice to be sent to someone in the wrong currency or may turn what is supposed to be an invoice into a credit note. While not major problems, usually, data that is erroneous may make the system fail.

User Error

This factor is an important contributor to system failure. If a user is improperly trained then the likelihood of them making serious errors is increased due to their lack of knowledge of the system. Failures due to a lack of training should not be thought of as an error due to the individual operator as is likely with a poorly designed user interface.

Hardware Errors

These failures are those that are primarily caused by hardware faults or by the entity not having the resources necessary to make the specified system usable.

These are faults such as:

- Damaged hardware,
- Badly designed hardware,
- A poor fit between the system and the organization.

Faulty Hardware

Faulty hardware is a problem that can cause severe system failure. It is also one that is hard to guard against. This factor is however an important one that should be given due consideration along with the more common software errors. An example of a hardware error in a system can be found in the experience of the Wide Field Infrared Explorer (WIRE) spacecraft operated by NASA.

FAULT TYPES

Faults are classified according to their **temporal behaviour** and **operation behaviour.** A fault is said to be active when it is physically capable of generating errors and to be **benign** when it is not.

Temporal Behaviour Classification

There are three fault types:

- Permanent Fault
- Intermittent Fault
- Transient Fault

A permanent fault does not die away with time, but remains until it is repaired or the affected unit is replaced.

An intermittent fault cycles between the fault-active and fault benign states.

A transient fault dies away after some time.

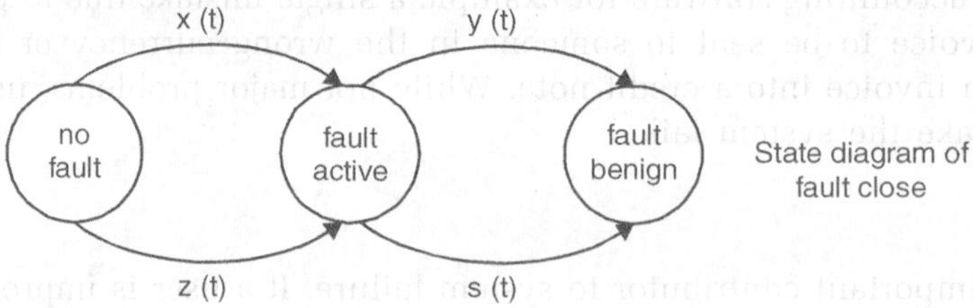

Fig. 4.2. *State diagram of fault classes.*

Fault type	*Condition*	
Permanent	x(t) > 0,	y(t) = z(t) = s(t) = 0
Transient	x(t) > 0	y(t) = 0, z(t) > 0, s(t) = 0
Intermittent	x(t) > 0	y(t) > 0, z(t) = 0, s(t) > 0

In the Fig. x(*t*) and y(*t*) are the rates at which the fault switches states and *t* is the age of the fault.

- A transient faults can be caused by environmental effects, for instance, if there is a burst of electromagnetic radiation and the memory is not properly shielded; the contents of the memory can be altered without the memory chips themselves suffering any structural damage. When the memory is rewritten, the fault will go away.
- Experiments suggest that the vast majority of hardware faults are transient and that only a minority are permanent.

- Transient failures are hard to catch, since quite often by the time the system has recognized that such a failure has occurred it has disappeared, leaving behind no permanent defect that can be located.
- It is likely that as devices become faster, their vulnerability to environmental effects that lead to transient failure will increase. This is because the principal way of making a device runfaster is to make it smaller, so that signal propagation times as well as the volume of charge required to switch a F/F from one state to the other is reduced. It therefore becomes more likely that a charged particale passing through a device or electromagnetic induction will cause a spurious change in the device state. This problem is especially serious in RTS that operate in hazardous environment that are replete with such radiation and such as a space.

Output Operation Behaviour Classification

- A fault is also characterized by the nature of the errors that it generates. There are two categories of operation behaviour:

  – Nonmalicious

  – Malicious.
- To understand the difference consider a unit A, which is providing operation to units B_1, ..., B_n. If 'A' has a normalicious fault, any error it generates will be interpreted in a consistent way by all of the units B_i.

  Example: If 'A' has an operation line that is stuck at logic 0. This is a nonmalicious fault because all the units that receive input from this line will read the line as producing a logic 0.
- Failures corresponding to an inconsistent operation are much harder to neutralize than the nonmalicious type. Indeed, we may think of them somewhat whimsically as the operation of some malicious intelligence that has captured the device and is putting forth errors in such a way as to cause maximum disruption to the function of the system. Such failures are known as **malicious (or) Byzantine** failures. In short, a malicious fault is one that is assumed to behave arbitrarily.

  The term's **fail-safe** and **fail-stop** can be defined.
- A unit is said to be **fail stop** if it responds to up to a certain maximum number of failures by simply stopping rather than putting out incorrect output. Fail stop units typically consist of multiple processors running the same tasks and comparing result. Faults are detected by comparing operations if the operations are different the whole unit turns itself off.
- A system said to be **fail-safe** if its failure mode is biased so that the application process does not suffer catastrophe upon failure. The classic example of a fail-safe system is a "traffic-light controller".

Independence and Correlation

Component failures may be independent of one another or correlated. A failure is said to be independent if it does not directly or indirecily cause another failure. Failures are said to be correlated if they are related in same way.

Example: They may be triggered by the same cause or one of them might cause the others to occur.

Failures can be correlated due to a physical or electrical coupling of units or because the same external event affects both units. Correlated failures are far more difficult to deal with than independent failures and means must be found to avoid them, if at all possible. Sometimes, the hardware is physically separated. So that the probability of multiple processors being affected by the same environmental event is reduced.

Example: The processors of an aircraft-control computer might be distributed among multiple instrument bays.

FAULT DETECTION

There are two ways to determine that a processor is malfunctioning: **online** and **offline.**

Online detection goes on in parallel with normal system operation. One way of doing this is to check for any behaviour *i.e.,* inconsistent with correct operation. The following actions are indicative of a faulty processor.

- Branching to an invalid destination.
- Fetching an operation code from a location containing data.
- Writing into a portion of memory to which the process has no write access.
- Fetching an illegal operation code.
- Inactive for more than a prescribed period.

A monitor (called a watchdog processor) is associated with each processor, looking for signs that the processor is faulty. The watchdog processor watches the data and addresslines as shown in Fig. 4.3. A second approach is to have multiple processors, which are supposed to put out the same result and compare the results. A discrepancy indicates the existence of a fault.

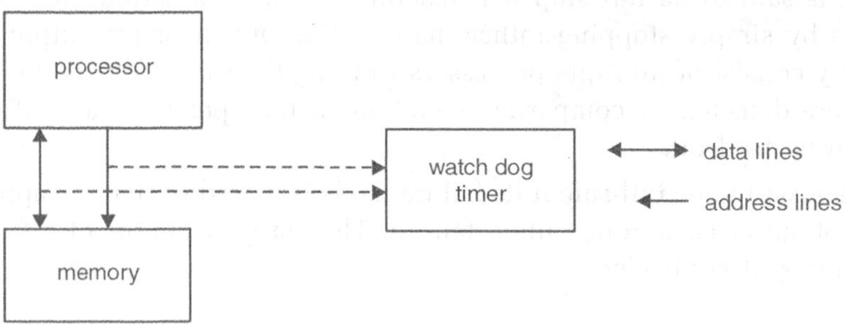

Fig. 4.3

Offline detection consists of running diagnostic tests. When a processor is running such a test, it obviously can't be executing the applications software. Diagnostic tests can be scheduled just like ordinary tasks. The greater the failure rate, the greater must be the frequency with which these tests are run.

FAULT AND ERROR CONTAINMENT

- When a fault or error occurs in one part of the system, it can if unchecked. Spread through the system like an infectious disease. A fault in one part of the system might. **Example:** Cause, large voltage swings in another a fault free processor can put out erroneous results as a result facing erroneous input from a faulty unit. Faults and errors must therefore be prevented from spreading through the system. This is called "Containment". The concept is an old one and has been widely used in other fields. **Example:** Ships have long been divided into separate watertight compartments so that damage to a small number of the compartments does not sink the ship. The system is divided into **fault and error-containment zones** (FCZ and ECZ).
- An FCZ is a subset of the system that operates correctly despite arbitrary logical and electrical faults outside the subset. *i.e.,* the failure of some part of the computer outside an **FCZ** can't cause any element inside that FCZ to fail. Hardware inside an **FCZ** must be isolated from hardware outside it. The isolation should be sufficiently robust to withstand either short-circuit or the application of the maximum voltage imposed on the lines connecting FCZ to the outside world.
- Each FCZ should have an independent power supply and its own clock. Typically, FCZ consists of a whole computers including processors, memory, input, ouput and control interfaces.
- The function of an ECZ is to prevent errors from across zone boundaries. This is typically achieved by voting and redundant output as shall see the next section.

REDUNDANCY

Fault-tolerance consists of using and properly managing redundancy. In other words, if the system is to kept running despite the failure of some of its parts, it must have spare capacity to begin with. There are four types of redundancy's.

- Hardware Redundnacy (H/WR)
- Software Redundancy (S/WR)
- Time Redundancy (TR)
- Unformation Redundancy (IR)

Hardware Redundancy

The system is provided with far more hardware than it would need if all the components were perfectly reliable typically, between two and three times as much.

Hardware redemdancy is the use of additional hardware to compensate for failure it can be used in two ways.

- The first is its use for fault detection, correction and masking.
- Multiple Hardware units may be assigned to do the same task in parallel and their results compared. If one or more of these units are faulting we can expect this to show up as a disagreement in the results. This is fault detection.
- Correction and masking are short-form measures. They neutralize the effects of the observed failure.
- The second and long term use of hardware redundancy is to replace the malfunctioning units. It is possible for systems to be designed so that spares can be switched in to replace any faulty units.

  These two ways complement each other. The extent to which they are employed depends on the nature of the application.
- Redundancy is expensive. Duplicating or triplicating hardware is a luxury *i.e.,* only Justified in the most critical applications. Traditionally, such use has been largely confined to aerospace applications. As computers are increasingly present in more cost-sensitive applications, such as automobiles, only the most critical functions can be allocated such High levels of redundancy. In aerospace and other applications, redundancy is more often limited by how much power consumption, heat dissipation or volume can be accommodated.

Software Redundancy

The system is provided with different software versions of tasks, preferably written independent by different teams of programmers, so that when one version of task fails under certain inputs, another version can be used.

Time Redundancy

The task schedule has some slacks in it, so that some tasks can be rerun if necessary and still meets critical deadlines.

Information Redundancy

The data are coded in such a way that a certain number of bit errors can be detected and or corrected.

INTEGRATED FAILURE HANDLING

When an error is detected, the system must respond swiftly to deal with it. In the short-term, the error might be masked by voting. In the long-term, the system will have to locate the failure that give rise to the error and decide what to do with fault unit. Three options are usually available: **retry, disconnect and replace.**

Instruction **retry** simply consists of retrying the failed instruction in the hope that the failure was caused by a transient fault, which has since gone away. To be able to do this. We need to be able to detect the error very quickly. If the error is detected after several further instructions have been executed. The question of which instruction caused the error is not easy to answer. To catch such errors, we need fast detection using **"signal-level detection"** mechanisms. Such mechanisms include error-detection codes, duplicated circuit with matchers and so on. These mechanisms are distinct from **"function-level detection"** mechanisms which operate at the function or module level and take much more time to catch an error.

- If we decide that the processor has suffered permanent failure, it must be disconnected from the rest of the system. This can be done by preventing it from communicating on the network or by ignoring its operation. If a processor is disconnected. We must find new processors to run the tasks that it was allocated.
- Replace is another way of responding to permanent failure. If spare processor is exist, they can be switched in to take the place of the failed unit. All the duties previously performed by the failed processor will now be transferred to the replacement. The replacement processor must have its memory updated suitably to allow it to undertake these computations and must have its clock synchronized with the rest of the system. There are several issues to take into account. When deciding which recovery action to follow. Four of these are:
  - Timing information.
  - Recovery time.
  - Probability of the recovery action succeeding.
  - State transition rates.

Timing Information

The overall aim is to meet the hard deadlines of the critical tasks. This is the ultimate test of success or failure and everything is subordinated to the need to maximize the probability of meeting such deadlines.

Recovery Time

This is connected with the probability of meeting hard deadlines. Different recovery mechanisms take different amounts of time and this therefore affects the choice of mechanism.

Probability of the Recovery Action Succeding

There is often a trade-off between low overhead and the probability of success. Instruction retry has perhaps the lowest overhead of all. If failure is a transient one of long duration or a permanent fault, it will not succeed. On the other hand, a recovery action that could have succeeded with little overhead but which was overlooked in favour of another Higher-overhead action represents a waste of time that can affect reliability and performance.

State Transition Rates

The rate at which failures occur will play a role in determining what recovery action to take.

In order to determine a response to failure, the system must be aware of the time taken by the various error-detection and failure handling mechanisms. Unfortunately, very little is known about these times in practice. This is an area that requires extensive systematic experimental research.

❑❑❑

Unit **5**

CASE STUDIES

- VX Works
  - Memory Managements
  - Task State Transition Diagram
  - Pre-emptive Priority
  - Scheduling
  - Context Swtiches—Semaphore—Binary Mutex, Counting
  - Watch Dogs, I/O System
- RT Linux
  - Process Management
  - Scheduling
  - Interrupt Management and Scynchronization

INTRODUCTION

Modern real-time systems are based on the complementary concepts of **multitasking** and **intertask communications**.

- A multitasking environment allows a real-time application to be constructed as a set of independent tasks, each with its own thread of execution and set of system resources.
- The intertask communication facilities allow these tasks to synchronize and communicate in order to coordinate their activities.
- In VxWorks, the intertask communication facilities range from fast semaphores to message queues and pipes to network-transparent sockets.

Another key facility in real-time systems is hardware interrupt handling, because interrupts are the usual mechanism to inform a system of external events. To get the fastest possible response to interrupts, *interrupt service routines (ISRs)* in **VxWorks** run in a special context of their own, outside of any task's context.

PROCESS MANAGEMENT

Scheduling Policy

There are only two scheduling policies available. Default is preemptive priority scheduling; it can be changed to Round-Robin scheduling. User can switch between these two polities during runtime.

Periodic Threads

There are no means to handle periodic threads. It is necessary for an application to use standard timers.

Range of Priorities and Maximum Number of Threads

There are 256 priority levels in range 0–255, 0 is the highest priority. Number of threads limited only by amount of available memory etc.

Thread Creation and Deletion

Threads can be created dynamically by calling TaskSpawn( ) function.

MEMORY MANAGEMENT

Protected Address Spaces

There is no any protection between user and system space and among different processes in basic VxWorks OS. All processes have unlimited access into whole memory space. Memory protection is available as optional package (VxVMI).

Dynamic Memory Allocation

Full support using standard functions malloc( ), calloc( ), realloc( ) and free( ).

Tasks

It is often essential to organize applications into independent, though cooperating, and programs. Each of these programs, while executing, is called a *task*. In VxWorks, tasks have immediate, shared access to most system resources, while also maintaining enough separate contexts to maintain individual threads of control.

MULTITASKING

Multitasking provides the fundamental mechanism for an application to control and react to multiple, discrete real-world events.

The VxWorks real-time kernel, *wind*, provides the basic multitasking environment. Multitasking creates the appearance of many threads of execution running concurrently when, in fact, the kernel interleaves their executions on the basis of a scheduling algorithm.

Each apparently independent program is called a *task*. Each task has its own ***context***, which is the CPU environment and system resources that the task sees each time it is scheduled to run by the kernel. On a context switch, a task's context is saved in the task control block (TCB). A task's context includes:

- a thread of execution, that is, the task's program counter.
- the CPU registers and (optionally) floating-point registers.
- a stack for dynamic variables and function calls.
- I/O assignments for standard input, output, and error.
- a delay timer.
- a timeslice timer.
- kernel control structures.
- signal handlers.
- debugging and performance monitoring values.

TASK STATE TRANSITION

The kernel maintains the current state of each task in the system. A task changes from one state to another as the result of kernel function calls made by the application. When created, tasks enter the suspended state. Activation is necessary for a created task to enter the ready state.

The activation phase is extremely fast, enabling applications to pre-create tasks and activate them in a timely manner. An alternative is the spawning primitive, which allows a task to be created and activated with a single function. Tasks can be deleted from any state.

The wind kernel states are shown in the state transition diagram in Figure 5.1, and a summary of the corresponding state symbols you will see when working with Tornado development tools is shown in Table 5.1.

Table 5.1. Task State Transitions

State Symbol	*Description*
READY	The state of a task that is not waiting for any resource other than the CPU.
PEND	The state of a task that is blocked due to the unavailability of some resources.
DELAY	The state of a task that is asleep for some durations.
SUSPEND	The state of a task that is unavailable for execution. This state is used primarily for debugging. Suspension does not inhibit state transition, only task execution.
DELAY + S	The state of a task that is both delayed and suspended.
PEND + S	The state of a task that is both pended and suspended.
PEND + T	The state of a task that is pended with a timeout value.
PEND + S + T	The state of a task that is both pended with a timeout value and suspended.
STATE + I	The state of task specified by state, plus an inherited priority.

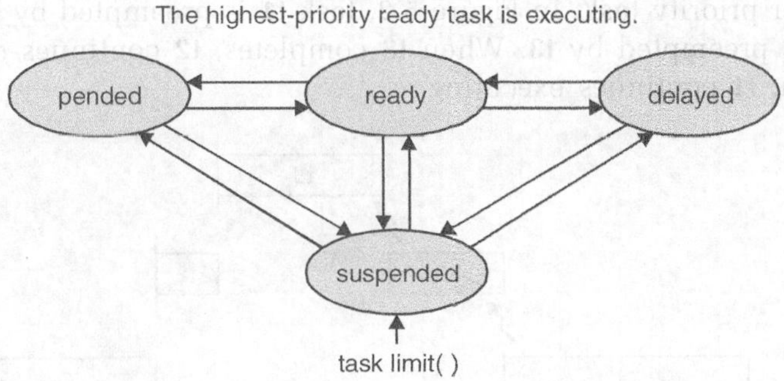

ready → pended		seinTake( ) / msg( )Receive( )
ready → delayed		taskDelay( )
ready → suspended		taskSuspend( )
pended → ready		seinGive( ) / msgQSend( )
pended → suspended		taskSuspend( )
delayed → ready		expired delay
delayed → suspended		taskSuspend( )
suspended → ready		taskResume( ) / taskActivate( )
suspended → pended		taskResume( )
suspended → delayed		taskResume( )

Fig. 5.1. *Task State Transitions.*

Wind Task Scheduling

- Multitasking requires a scheduling algorithm to allocate the CPU to ready tasks.
- **Priority-based preemptive scheduling** is the default algorithm in wind, but you can select round-robin scheduling for your applications as well.
- The routines listed in Table 5.2 control task scheduling.

Table 5.2. Task Scheduler Control Routines

Call	*Description*
kernelTimeSlice( )	Control round-robin scheduling.
taskPrioritySet( )	Change the priority of a task.
taskLock( )	Disable task rescheduling.
taskUnlock( )	Enable task rescheduling.

PREEMPTIVE PRIORITY SCHEDULING

With a preemptive priority-based scheduler, each task has a priority and the kernel ensures that the CPU is allocated to the highest priority task that is ready to run. This scheduling method is preemptive in that if a task that has higher priority than the current task becomes ready to run, the kernel immediately saves the current task's context and switches to the context of the higher priority task. In Figure 5.2, task **t1** is preempted by higher-priority task **t2**, which in turn is preempted by **t3**. When **t3** completes, **t2** continues executing. When **t2** completes execution, **t1** continues executing.

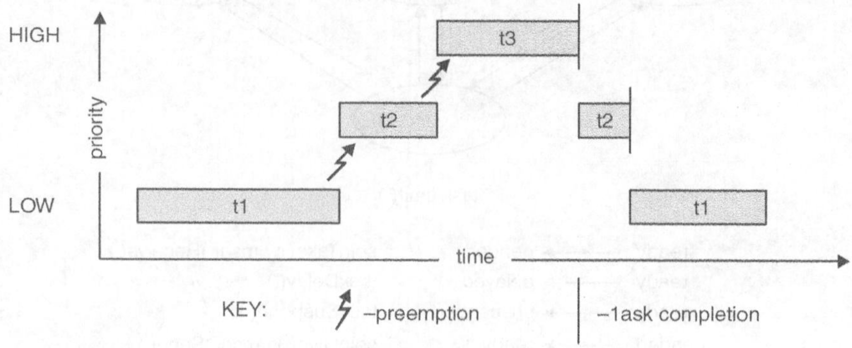

Fig. 5.2. *Priority Preemption.*

The wind kernel has 256 priority levels, numbered 0 through 255. Priority 0 is the highest and priority 255 is the lowest. Tasks are assigned a priority when created; however, while executing, a task can change its priority using **taskPrioritySet( )**. The ability to change task priorities dynamically allows applications to track precedence changes in the real world.

ROUND-ROBIN SCHEDULING

Preemptive priority scheduling can be augmented with round-robin scheduling. A round-robin scheduling algorithm attempts to share the CPU fairly among all ready tasks of the same priority. Without round-robin scheduling, when multiple tasks of equal priority must share the processor, a single task can usurp the processor by never blocking, thus never giving other equal-priority tasks a chance to run.

Round-robin scheduling achieves fair allocation of the CPU to tasks of the same priority by an approach known as time slicing. Each task of a group of tasks executes for a defined interval, or time slice; then another task executes for an equal interval, in rotation. The allocation is fair in that no task of a priority group gets a second slice of time before the other tasks of a group are given a slice.

Round-robin scheduling can be enabled with the routine **kernelTimeSlice( )**, which takes a parameter for a time slice, or interval. This interval is the amount of time each task is allowed to run before relinquishing the processor to another equal-priority task.

More precisely, a run-time counter is kept for each task and incremented on every clock tick.

When the specified time-slice interval is completed, the counter is cleared and the task is placed at the tail of the queue of tasks at its priority. New tasks joining a priority group are placed at the tail of the group with a run-time counter initialized to zero.

If a task is preempted by a higher priority task during its interval, its run-time count is saved and then restored when the task is again eligible for execution. Figure 5.3 shows round-robin scheduling for three tasks of the same priority: **t1**, **t2**, and **t3**. Task **t2** is preempted by a higher priority task **t4**, but resumes at the count, where it left off when **t4** is finished.

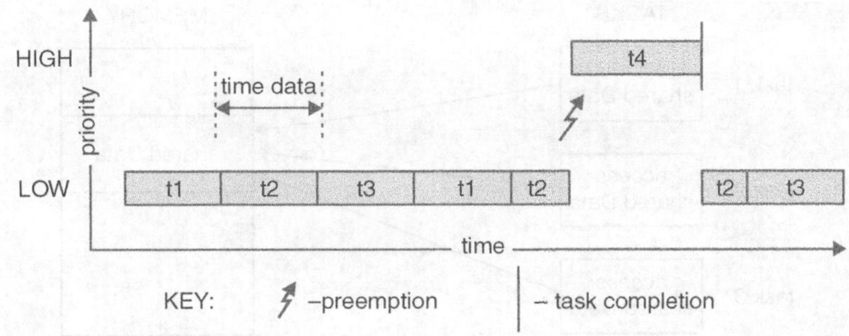

Fig. 5.3. *Round-Robin Scheduling.*

Preemption Locks

The wind scheduler can be explicitly disabled and enabled on a per-task basis with the routines **taskLock( )** and **taskUnlock( )**. When a task disables the scheduler by calling **taskLock( )**, no priority-based preemption can take place while that task is running.

However, if the task explicitly blocks or suspends, the scheduler selects the next highest-priority eligible task to execute. When the preemption-locked task unblocks and begins running again, preemption is again disabled.

NOTE *That preemption locks prevent task context switching but do not lock out interrupt handling.*

Preemption locks can be used to achieve mutual exclusion; however, keep the duration of preemption locking to a minimum.

VxWorks having a set of **intertask communication mechanisms,** including:

- ***Shared memory***, for simple sharing of data.
- ***Semaphores***, for basic mutual exclusion and synchronization.
- ***Message queues*** and ***pipes***, for intertask message passing within a CPU.
- ***Sockets*** and ***remote procedure calls***, for network-transparent intertask communication.
- ***Signals***, for exception handling.

Shared Data Structures

The most obvious way for tasks to communicate is by accessing shared data structures. Because, all tasks in VxWorks exist in a single linear address space, sharing data structures between tasks is trivial; see Figure 5.4.

Global variables, linear buffers, ring buffers, linked lists, and pointers can be referenced directly by code running in different contexts.

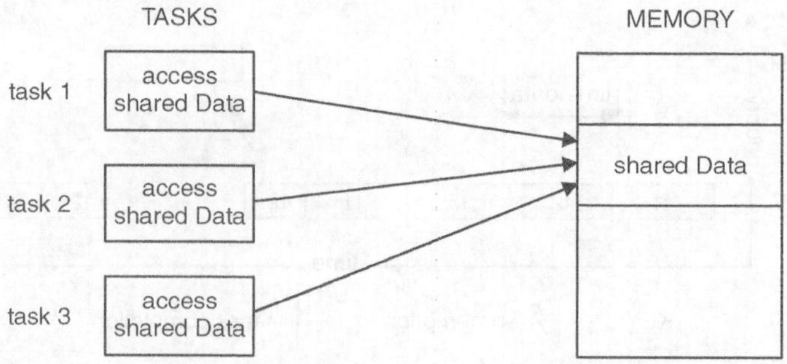

Fig. 5.4. *Shared Data Structures.*

Mutual Exclusion

While a shared address space simplifies exchange of data, **interlocking** access to memory is crucial to avoid contention. Many methods exist for obtaining exclusive access to resources, and vary only in the scope of the exclusion. Such methods include disabling interrupts, disabling preemption, and resource locking with semaphores.

Interrupt Locks and Latency

The most powerful method available for mutual exclusion is the disabling of interrupts. Such a lock guarantees exclusive access to the CPU:

```
funcA()
{
    . int lock = intLock();
    . critical region that cannot be interrupted
    . intUnlock (lock);
}
```

While this solves problems involving mutual exclusion with ISRs, it is inappropriate as a general-purpose mutual-exclusion method for most real-time systems, because it prevents the system from responding to external events for the duration of these locks. Interrupt latency is unacceptable whenever an immediate response to an external event is required. Interrupt locking can sometimes be necessary, where mutual exclusion involves ISRs. In any situation, keep the duration of interrupt lockouts short.

Preemptive Locks and Latency

Disabling preemption offers a somewhat less restrictive form of mutual exclusion. While no other task is allowed to preempt the current executing task, ISRs are able to execute:

```
funcA( )
{
    taskLock( );
```

```
. critical region that cannot be interrupted
        . taskUnlock ();
    }
```

However, this method can lead to unacceptable real-time response. Tasks of higher priority are unable to execute until the locking task leaves the critical region, even though the higher-priority task is not itself involved with the critical region. While this kind of mutual exclusion is simple, if you use it, make sure to keep the duration short. A better mechanism is provided by semaphores.

SEMAPHORES

VxWorks semaphores are highly optimized and provide the fastest intertask communication mechanism in VxWorks.

Semaphores are the primary means for addressing the requirements of both **mutual exclusion** and **task synchronization**:

- For ***mutual exclusion***, semaphores interlock access to shared resources. They provide mutual exclusion with finer granularity than either interrupt disabling or preemptive locks.
- For ***synchronization***, semaphores coordinate a task's execution with external events.

There are **three** types of **Wind semaphores**, optimized to address different classes of problems:

Binary

The fastest, most general-purpose semaphore. Optimized for synchronization or mutual exclusion.

Mutual Exclusion

A special binary semaphore optimized for problems inherent in mutual exclusion: priority inheritance, deletion safety, and recursion.

Counting

Like the binary semaphore, but keeps track of the number of times a semaphore is given. Optimized for guarding multiple instances of a resource.

BINARY SEMAPHORES

The general-purpose binary semaphore is capable of addressing the requirements of both forms of task coordination: **mutual exclusion** and **synchronization**. The binary semaphore has the least overhead associated with it, making it particularly applicable to high-performance requirements. The mutual-exclusion semaphore described in ***Mutual-Exclusion Semaphores*** is also a **binary semaphore**, but it has been optimized to address problems inherent to mutual exclusion. Alternatively, the binary semaphore can be used for mutual exclusion if the advanced features of the mutual-exclusion semaphore are deemed unnecessary.

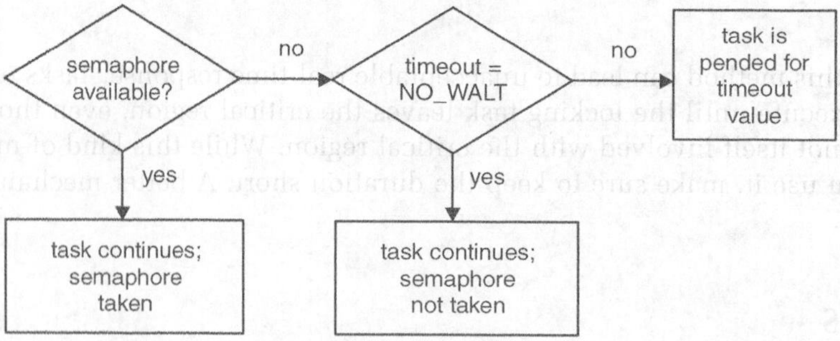

Fig. 5.5. *Taking a Semaphore.*

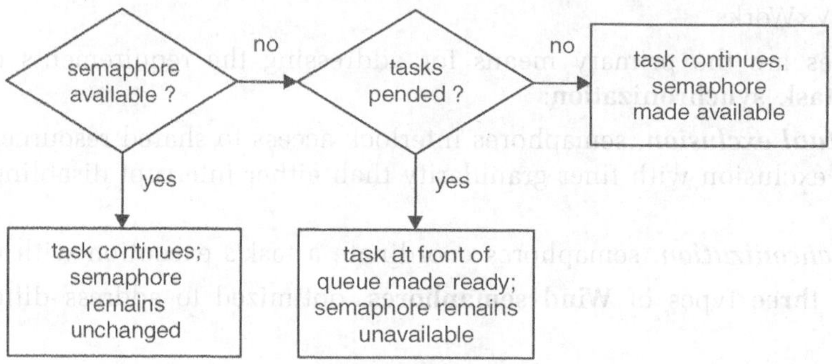

Fig. 5.6. *Giving a Semaphore.*

A binary semaphore can be viewed as a flag that is available (full) or unavailable (empty). When a task takes a binary semaphore, with ***semTake( )***, the outcome depends on whether the semaphore is available (full) or unavailable (empty) at the time of the call; see Figure 5-5. If the semaphore is available (full), the semaphore becomes unavailable (empty) and the task continues executing immediately. If the semaphore is unavailable (empty), the task is put on a queue of blocked tasks and enters a state of pending on the availability of the semaphore.

When a task gives a binary semaphore, using ***semGive( )***, the outcome also depends on whether the semaphore is available (full) or unavailable (empty) at the time of the call; see Figure 5.6. If the semaphore is already available (full), giving the semaphore has no effect at all. If the semaphore is unavailable (empty) and no task is waiting to take it, then the semaphore becomes available (full). If the semaphore is unavailable (empty) and one or more tasks are pending on its availability, then the first task in the queue of blocked tasks is unblocked, and the semaphore is left unavailable (empty).

Mutual Exclusion

Binary semaphores interlock access to a shared resource efficiently. Unlike disabling interrupts or preemptive locks, binary semaphores limit the scope of the mutual exclusion to only the associated resource. In this technique, a semaphore is created to guard the resource. Initially the semaphore is available (full).

```
/* includes */
#include "vxWorks.h"
#include "semLib.h"

SEM_ID semMutex;

/* Create a binary semaphore that is initially full. Tasks *
 * blocked on semaphore wait in priority order.          */

semMutex = semBCreate (SEM_Q_PRIORITY, SEM_FULL);
```

When a task wants to access the resource, it must first take that semaphore. As long as the task keeps the semaphore, all other tasks seeking access to the resource are blocked from execution. When the task is finished with the resource, it gives back the semaphore, allowing another task to use the resource.

Thus, all accesses to a resource requiring mutual exclusion are bracketed with ***semTake( )*** and ***semGive( )*** pairs:

```
semTake (semMutex, WAIT_FOREVER);
.
. critical region, only accessible by a single task at a time
.
semGive (semMutex);
```

Synchronization

When used for task synchronization, a semaphore can represent a condition or event that a task is waiting for. Initially the semaphore is unavailable (empty). A task or ISR signals the occurrence of the event by giving the semaphore. Another task waits for the semaphore by calling ***semTake( )***. The waiting task blocks until the event occurs and the semaphore is given.

Note the difference in sequence between semaphores used for mutual exclusion and those used for synchronization. For mutual exclusion, the semaphore is initially full, and each task first takes, and then gives back the semaphore. For synchronization, the semaphore is initially empty, and one task waits to take the semaphore given by another task.

In Example 5.1, the ***init( )*** routine creates the binary semaphore, attaches an ISR to an event, and spawns a task to process the event. The routine ***task1( )*** runs until it calls ***semTake( )***. It remains blocked at that point until an event causes the ISR to call ***semGive( )***. When the ISR completes, ***task1( )*** executes to process the event. There is an advantage of handling event processing within the context of a dedicated task: less processing takes place at interrupt level, thereby reducing interrupt latency. This model of event processing is recommended for real-time applications.

Example 5.1: Using Semaphores for Task Synchronization

```
/* This example shows the use of semaphores for task synchronization. */

/* includes */
#include "vxWorks.h"
#include "semLib.h"
#include "arch/arch/ivarch.h" /* replace arch with architecture type */

SEM_ID syncSem;       /* ID of sync semaphore */

init (
    int someIntNum
    )
    {
    /* connect interrupt service routine */
    intConnect (INUM_TO_IVEC (someIntNum), eventInterruptSvcRout, 0);

    /* create semaphore */
    syncSem = semBCreate (SEM_Q_FIFO, SEM_EMPTY);

    /* spawn task used for synchronization. */
    taskSpawn ("sample", 100, 0, 20000, task1, 0,0,0,0,0,0,0,0,0,0);
    }

task1 (void)
    {
    ...
    semTake (syncSem, WAIT_FOREVER); /* wait for event to occur */
    printf ("task 1 got the semaphore\n");
    ... /* process event */
    }

eventInterruptSvcRout (void)
    {
    ...
    semGive (syncSem);  /* let task 1 process event */
    ...
    }
```

Broadcast synchronization allows all processes that are blocked on the same semaphore to be unblocked atomically. Correct application behaviour often requires a set of tasks to process an event before any task of the set has the opportunity to process further events. The routine ***semFlush*( )** addresses this class of synchronization problem by unblocking all tasks pended on a semaphore.

Mutual-Exclusion Semaphores

The mutual-exclusion semaphore is a specialized binary semaphore designed to address issues inherent in mutual exclusion, including priority inversion, deletion safety, and recursive access to resources.

The fundamental behaviour of the mutual-exclusion semaphore is identical to the binary semaphore, with the following exceptions:

- It can be used only for mutual exclusion.
- It can be given only by the task that took it.
- It cannot be given from an ISR.
- The ***semFlush*( )** operation is illegal.

Priority Inversion

Priority inversion arises when a higher-priority task is forced to wait an indefinite period of time for a lower-priority task to complete. Consider the scenario in Figure 5.7: **t1**, **t2**, and **t3** are tasks of high, medium, and low priority, respectively. **t3** has acquired some resource by taking its associated binary guard semaphore. When **t1** preempts **t3** and contends for the resource by taking the same semaphore, it becomes blocked. If we could be assured that **t1** would be blocked no longer than the time it normally takes **t3** to finish with the resource, there would be no problem, because the resource cannot be preempted. However, the low-priority task is vulnerable to preemption by medium-priority tasks (like **t2**), which could inhibit **t3** from relinquishing the resource. This condition could persist, blocking **t1** for an indefinite period of time.

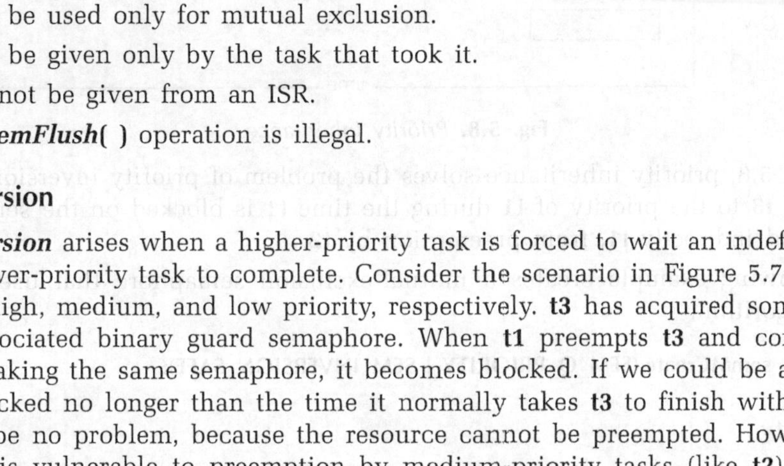

Fig. 5.7. *Priority Inversion.*

The mutual-exclusion semaphore has the option **SEM_INVERSION_SAFE**, which enables a *priority-inheritance* algorithm. The priority-inheritance protocol assures that a task that owns a resource executes at the priority of the highest-priority task blocked on that resource. Once the task priority has been elevated, it remains at the higher level until all mutual-exclusion semaphores that the task owns are released; then the task returns to its normal, or standard, priority. Hence, the "inheriting" task is protected from preemption by any intermediate-priority tasks. This option must be used in conjunction with a priority queue (**SEM_Q_PRIORITY**).

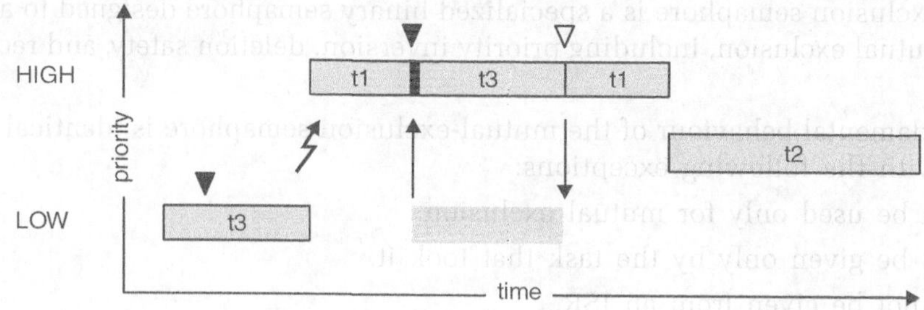

Fig. 5.8. *Priority Inheritance.*

In Figure 5.8, priority inheritance solves the problem of priority inversion by elevating the priority of **t3** to the priority of **t1** during the time **t1** is blocked on the semaphore. This protects **t3**, and indirectly **t1**, from preemption by **t2**.

The following example creates a mutual-exclusion semaphore that uses the priority inheritance algorithm:

```
semId = semMCreate (SEM_Q_PRIORITY | SEM_INVERSION_SAFE);
```

Deletion Safety

Another problem of mutual exclusion involves task deletion. Within a critical region guarded by semaphores, it is often desirable to protect the executing task from unexpected deletion. Deleting a task executing in a critical region can be catastrophic. The resource might be left in a corrupted state and the semaphore guarding the resource left unavailable, effectively preventing all access to the resource.

The primitives ***taskSafe*( )** and ***taskUnsafe*( )** provide one solution to task deletion. However, the mutual-exclusion semaphore offers the option **SEM_DELETE_SAFE**, which enables an implicit ***taskSafe*( )** with each ***semTake*( )**, and a ***taskUnsafe*( )** with each ***semGive*( )**. In this way, a task can be protected from deletion while it has the semaphore. This option is more efficient than the primitives ***taskSafe*( )** and ***taskUnsafe*( )**, as the resulting code requires fewer entrances to the kernel.

```
semId = semMCreate (SEM_Q_FIFO | SEM_DELETE_SAFE);
```

Recursive Resource Access

Mutual-exclusion semaphores can be taken ***recursively***. This means that the semaphore can be taken more than once by the task that owns it before finally being released. Recursion is useful for a set of routines that must call each other but that also require mutually exclusive access to a resource. This is possible because the system keeps track of which task currently owns the mutual-exclusion semaphore.

Before being released, a mutual-exclusion semaphore taken recursively must be *given* the same number of times it is *taken*. This is tracked by a count that increments with each ***semTake***( ) and decrements with each ***semGive***( ).

Example 5.2: Recursive Use of a Mutual-Exclusion Semaphore

```
/* Function A requires access to a resource which it acquires by taking
 * mySem; function A may also need to call function B, which also
 * requires mySem:
/* includes */
#include "vxWorks.h"
#include "semLib.h"
SEM_ID mySem;

/* Create a mutual-exclusion semaphore. */
 init( )
   {
   mySem = semMCreate (SEM_Q_PRIORITY);
   }
funcA( )
   {
   semTake (mySem, WAIT_FOREVER);
   printf ("funcA: Got mutual-exclusion semaphore\n");
   ...
   funcB( );
   ...
   semGive (mySem);
   printf ("funcA: Released mutual-exclusion semaphore\n");
   }
funcB( )
   {
   semTake (mySem, WAIT_FOREVER);
   printf ("funcB: Got mutual-exclusion semaphore\n");
      semGive (mySem);
   printf ("funcB: Releases mutual-exclusion semaphore\n");
   }
```

COUNTING SEMAPHORES

Counting semaphores are another means to implement task synchronization and mutual exclusion. The counting semaphore works like the binary semaphore except that it keeps track of the number of times a semaphore is given. Every time a semaphore is given, the count is incremented; every time a semaphore is taken, the count is decremented. When the count reaches zero, a task that tries to take the semaphore is blocked. As with the binary semaphore, if a semaphore is given and a task is blocked, it becomes unblocked. However, unlike the binary semaphore, if a semaphore is given and no tasks are blocked, then the count is incremented. This means that a semaphore that is given twice can be taken twice without blocking. Table 5.3 shows an example time sequence of tasks taking and giving a counting semaphore that was initialized to a count of 3.

Table 5.3. Counting Semaphore Example

Semaphore	*Call-Count after Call*	*Resulting Behavior*
semCCreate( )	3	Semaphore initialized with initial count of 3.
semTake( )	2	Semaphore taken.
semTake( )	1	Semaphore taken.
semTake( )	0	Semaphore taken.
semTake( )	0	Task blocks waiting for semaphore to be available.
semGive( )	0	Task waiting is given semaphore.
semGive( )	1	No task waiting for semaphore; count incremented.

Counting semaphores are useful for guarding multiple copies of resources. For example, the use of five tape drives might be coordinated using a counting semaphore with an initial count of 5, or a ring buffer with 256 entries might be implemented using a counting semaphore with an initial count of 256. The initial count is specified as an argument to the ***semCCreate( )*** routine.

WATCHDOG TIMERS

VxWorks includes a watchdog-timer mechanism that allows any C function to be connected to a specified time delay. Watchdog timers are maintained as part of the system clock **ISR**. Normally, functions invoked by watchdog timers execute as interrupt service code at the interrupt level of the system clock. However, if the kernel is unable to execute the function immediately for any reason (such as a previous interrupt or kernel state), the function is placed on the **tExcTask** work queue. Functions on the **tExcTask** work queue execute at the priority level of the **tExcTask** (usually 0). Restrictions on ISRs apply to routines connected to watchdog timers. The functions in Table 5.4 are provided by the **wdLib** library.

Table 5.4. Watchdog Timer Calls

Call	*Description*
wdCreate( )	Allocate and initialize a watchdog timer.
wdDelete( )	Terminate and deallocate a watchdog timer.
wdStart( )	Start a watchdog timer.
wdCancel( )	Cancel a currently counting watchdog timer.

A watchdog timer is first created by calling **wdCreate( )**. Then the timer can be started by calling **wdStart( )**, which takes as arguments the number of ticks to delay, the C function to call, and an argument to be passed to that function. After the specified number of ticks have elapsed, the function is called with the specified argument. The watchdog timer can be canceled any time before the delay has elapsed by calling **wdCancel( )**.

Example 5.3: Watchdog Timers

```
/* This example creates a watchdog timer and sets it to go off in
 * 3 seconds.
 */ includes */
#include "vxWorks.h"
#include "logLib.h"
#include "wdLib.h"
/* defines */
#define SECONDS (3)
WDOG_ID myWatchDogId;
task (void)
  {
  /* Create watchdog */
   if ((myWatchDogId = wdCreate( )) = = NULL)
     return (ERROR);
  /* Set timer to go off in SECONDS - printing a message to stdout */
  if (wdStart (myWatchDogId, sysClkRateGet( ) * SECONDS, logMsg,
           "Watchdog timer just expired\n") = = ERROR)
     return (ERROR);
  /* ... */
```

I/O SYSTEM

The VxWorks I/O system is designed to present a simple, uniform, device-independent interface to any kind of device, including:

- character-oriented devices such as terminals or communications lines.
- random-access block devices such as disks.
- virtual devices such as intertask *pipes* and *sockets*.
- monitor and control devices such as digital/analog I/O devices.
- network devices that give access to remote devices.

The VxWorks **I/O system** provides uniform device-independent access to many kinds of devices. You can call **seven basic I/O** routines:

- ***creat***( ) Create a file.
- ***remove***( ) Remove a file.
- ***open***( ) Open a file (Optionally, create a file.)
- ***close***( ) Close a file.
- ***read***( ) Read a previously created or opened file.
- ***write***( ) Write a previously created or opened file.
- ***ioctl***( ) Perform special control functions on files.

Higher-level I/O routines (such as ANSI C-compatible ***printf***( ) and ***scanf***( ) routines) are also provided.

VxWorks also provides a standard buffered I/O package (*stdio*) that includes ANSI C-compatible routines such as ***fopen***( ), ***fclose***( ), ***fread***( ), ***fwrite***( ), ***getc***( ), and ***putc***( ). These routines increase I/O performance in many cases.

The VxWorks I/O system also includes POSIX-compliant asynchronous I/O: a library of routines that perform input and output operations concurrently with a task's other activities.

VxWorks includes device drivers for serial communication, disks, RAM disks, SCSI tape devices, intertask communication devices (called *pipes*), and devices on a network. Application developers can easily write additional drivers, if needed. VxWorks allows dynamic installation and removal of drivers without rebooting the system.

Internally, the VxWorks I/O system allows individual drivers complete control over how the user requests are serviced. Drivers can easily implement different protocols, unique device-specific routines, and even different file systems, without interference from the I/O system itself. VxWorks also supplies several high-level packages that make it easy for drivers to implement common device protocols and file systems.

- **Distinguishing features**
  - efficient POSIX-compliant memory management.
  - multiprocessor facilities.
  - shell for user interface.
  - symbolic and source level debugging capabilities.
  - performance monitoring.
- Mars Exploration Rovers *Spirit* and *Opportunity* and the Mars Reconnaissance Orbiter use the VxWorks operating system.

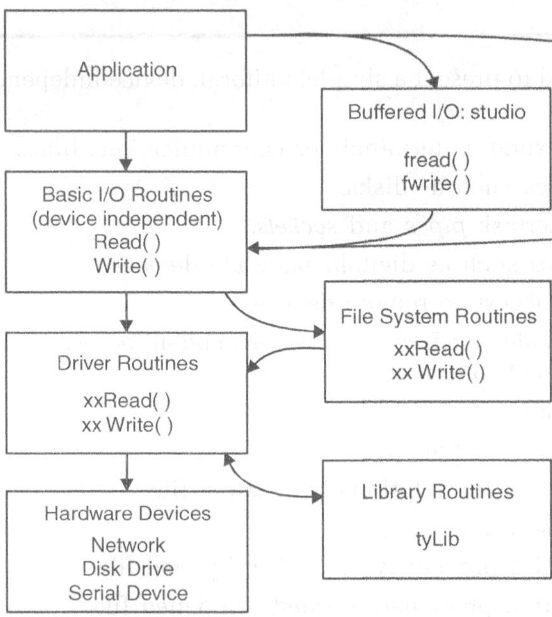

Fig. 5.9

INTRODUCTION TO RTLINUX

There are **two** different versions of RTLinux:

1. RTLinux/Pro
2. RTLinux/Open.

RTLinux/Open is available on the web. The main (only) developer of this version was FSMLabs and stops its development in 2Q/2001. RTLinux/Pro is available for a free from FSMLabs and the license is non-GPL.

This paper is focused of the RTLinux/Open version.

ARCHITECTURE OVERVIEW

There are two approaches to provide real-time performance in a Linux system:

1. Improving the Linux kernel preemption.
2. Adding a new software layer beneath Linux kernel with full control of interrupts and processor key features.

These two approaches are known as "***preemption improvement***" and "**interrupt abstraction**" respectively. This second approach is the one used by RTLinux.

RTLinux is a small, fast operating system, following the POSIX 1003.13 "**minimal real-time operating system**" standard.

RTLinux adds a layer of virtual hardware between the standard Linux kernel and the computer hardware (see Figure 5.10). As far as the standard Linux kernel is concerned, this new layer appears to be the actual hardware. RTLinux implements a complete and predictable

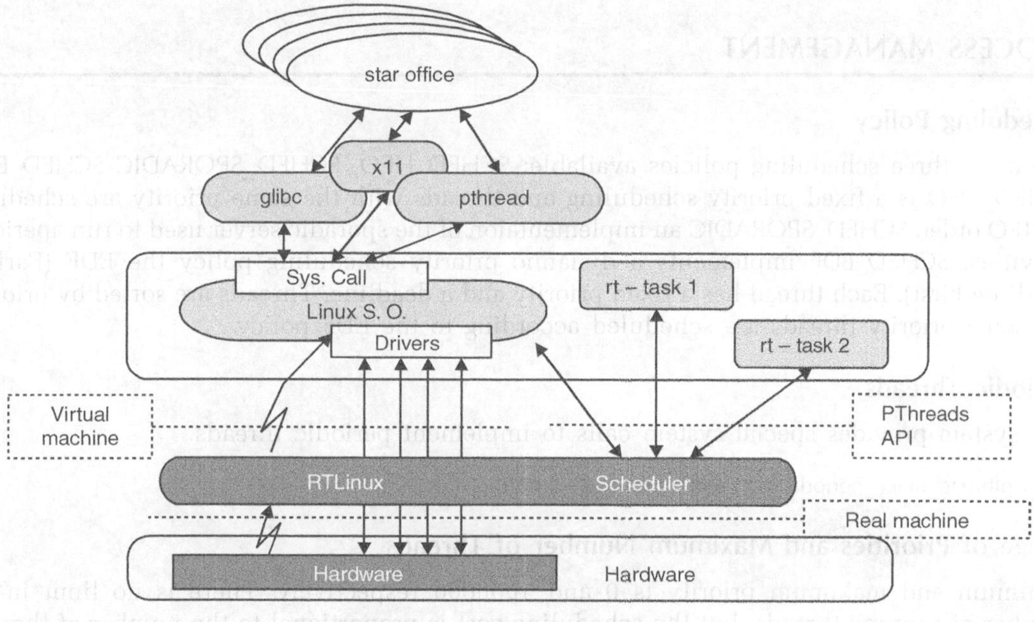

Fig. 5.10. *RTLinux layer architecture.*

RTOS with no interference from the non-real-time Linux. The RTLinux threads are executed directly by a fixed-priority scheduler. The whole Linux kernel, and all the normal Linux processes, are managed by the RTLinux scheduler as the background task. This way, it is possible to have a complete general purpose operating system running on top of a small predictable RTOS.

There are three main modifications done to the Linux kernel in order to virtualize the hardware so that RTLinux can take full control of the machine: The RTLinux layer takes direct control of all the hardware interrupts, interrupts that are not controlled by real-time threads are forwarded to the Linux upper level; RTLinux also takes the control of the timer hardware (8254 and APIC when available) and implements a virtual timer to Linux; and the last modification done to Linux to remove the basic control of the hardware from Linux is to replace all the cli and sti (disable and enable interrupt flag) functions calls from the Linux kernel so that Linux can no make a real disable but a virtual interrupt disable. These modifications are quiet complex and tricky, but do not require large code (Linux) modifications.

RTLinux provides an execution environment "below" the Linux kernel. One consequence of this, is that real-time threads can not use Linux services because deadlock or system inconsistencies may happen. To overcome this problem, the real-time system has to be divided into two separated layers: the hard real-time layer, executed on top of RTLinux, and the soft real-time, executed as normal Linux processes.

Several mechanisms (FIFO, shared memory) can be used to communicate threads in both layers.

The two layer approach is a useful method to provide hard real-time while having all the features of a desktop operating system. It decouples the mechanism of the real-time kernel from the mechanism of the general purpose Linux kernel so that each system can be optimized independently.

PROCESS MANAGEMENT

Scheduling Policy

There are three scheduling policies available: SCHED_FIFO, SCHED_SPORADIC SCHED_EDF. SCHED_FIFO is a fixed priority scheduling and threads with the same priority are scheduled in FIFO order. SCHED_SPORADIC an implementaion of the sporadic server used to run aperiodic activities. SCHED_EDF implements a dynamic priority scheduling policy the EDF (Earliest Deadline First). Each thread has a fixed priority and a deadline. Threads are sorted by priority, but same priority threads are scheduled according to the EDF policy.

Periodic Threads

The system provides special system calls to implement periodic threads.

pthread_make_periodic_np() and pthread_wait_np()

Range of Priorities and Maximum Number of Threads

Minimum and maximum priority is 0 and 1000000 respectively. There is no limit in the number of running threads, but the scheduling cost is proportional to the number of threads. Current scheduler code is designed to handle efficiently a low number of threads (around 10).

Thread Creation and Deletion

It provides all the POSIX Thread termination facilities and also some extensions to remove terminate threads easier.

A thread can terminate itself by calling pthread_exit( ) function. pthread_join( ) suspend execution the execution of the calling thread until the target thread terminates. To implement this behaviour, when a thread exits, the system do not delete the supporting data until other thread has *joined*. The system also provides the pthread_detach( ) function to indicate that the target thread will not be joined and the system support data can be reclaimed as soon as the thread exits.

A thread can request the cancellation (termination) of other thread: pthread_cancel( ). The thread that receives the cancellation request, depending on the *cancelability state*, can do one o the following action:

- PTHREAD_CANCEL_DISABLE: The cancel request is ignored.
- PTHREAD_CANCEL_DEFERRED: The thread will be canceled but only at some safe points.
- PTHREAD_CANCEL_ASYNCHRONOUS: The thread is canceled immediately.

A thread can install cancellation cleanup handlers: pthread_cleanup_push( ) and pthread_cleanup_pop( ). The cleanup handlers are called when the thread exits, is canceled or the handler is removed.

pthread_delete_np( ) function can be used to termintate inmediately a thread and can be used instead of the pair: pthread_cancel( )/pthread_join( )

MEMORY MANAGEMENT

Protected Address Spaces

Although, RTLinux is designed to run in processors with MMU, all the application threads and the RTLinux kernel run in the same address space.

There is no memory protection between threads and the kernel and also between threads themselves.

From the point of view of memory management, RTLinux is the *guest* operating system of the Linux Kernel. The Linux kernel has the whole control of the memory.

Dynamic Memory Allocation

RTLinux do not provide dynamic memory allocation nor use it internally. The main argument is that dynamic memory allocation is not predictable if implemented efficiently. The Real-Time goal of predictability is usually achieved by preallocating most of the resources the threads will use at run time. It is possible to allocate all the memory that each thread will require before the threads are created.

SCHEDULING

Priority Inversion

In scheduling, **priority inversion** is the scenario where a low priority task holds a shared resource that is required by a high priority task. This causes the execution of the high priority task to be blocked until the low priority task has released the resource, effectively "inverting" the relative priorities of the two tasks. If some other medium priority tasks that do not depend on the shared resource attempts to run in the interim, it will take precedence over both the **low priority task** and the **high priority task.**

In some cases, priority inversion can occur without causing immediate harm—the delayed execution of the high priority task goes unnoticed, and eventually the low priority task releases the shared resource. However, there are also many situations in which priority inversion can cause serious problems. If the high priority task is left starved of the resources, it might lead to a system malfunction or the triggering of predefined corrective measures, such as a watch dog timer resetting the entire system.

Priority inversion can also reduce the perceived performance of the system. Low priority tasks usually have a low priority because it is not important for them to finish promptly (for example, they might be a batch job or another non-interactive activity). Similarly, a high priority task has a high priority, because it is more likely to be subject to strict time constraints—it may be providing data to an interactive user, or acting subject to real-time Response guarantees. Because priority inversion results in the execution of the low priority task blocking the high priority task, it can lead to reduced system responsiveness, or even the violation of response time guarantees.

The existence of this problem has been known since the 1970s, but there is no fool-proof method to predict the situation. There are however many existing solutions, of which the most common ones are:

Disabling all Interrupts to Protect Critical Sections

When disabled interrupts are used to prevent priority inversion, there are only **two priorities:** ***preemptible,*** **and** ***interrupts disabled.*** With no third priority, inversion is impossible. Since there's only one piece of lock data (the interrupt-enable bit), misordering locking is impossible, and so deadlocks cannot occur. Since, the critical regions always run to completion, hangs do not occur. Note that this only works if all interrupts are disabled. If only a particular hardware device's interrupt is disabled, priority inversion is reintroduced by the hardware's prioritization of interrupts. A simple variation, "single shared-flag locking" is used on some systems with multiple CPUs. This scheme provides a single flag in shared memory that is used by all CPUs to lock all interprocessor critical sections with a busy-wait. Interprocessor communications are expensive and slow on most multiple CPU systems. Therefore, most such systems are designed to minimize shared resources. As a result, this scheme actually works well on many practical systems. These methods are widely used in simple embedded systems, where they are prized for their reliability, simplicity and low resources use. These schemes also require clever programming to keep the critical sections very brief, under 100 microseconds in practical systems. Many software engineers consider them impractical in general-purpose computers.

Arguably, these methods are similar to priority ceilings.

A Priority Ceiling

With priority ceilings, the shared mutex process (that runs the operating system code) has a characteristic (high) priority of its own, which is assigned to the task locking the mutex. This works well, provided the other high priority task(s) that try to access the mutex does not have a priority higher than the ceiling priority.

Priority Inheritance

When priority is inherited, the low priority task inherits the priority of the high priority task, thus stopping the medium priority task from pre-empting the high priority task.

INTERRUPT LATENCY

Interrupt latency is the time between the generation of an interrupt by a device and the servicing of the device which generated the interrupt. For many operating systems, devices are serviced as soon as the device's interrupt handler is executed. Interrupt latency may be affected by interrupt controllers, interrupt masking, and the operating system's (OS) interrupt handling methods.

Background

There is usually a tradeoff between interrupt latency, throughout and processor utilization. Many of the techniques of CPU and OS design that improve interrupt latency will decrease throughput and increase processor utilization. Techniques that increase throughput may increase interrupt latency and increase processor utilization. Lastly, trying to reduce processor utilization may increase interrupt latency and decrease throughput.

Minimum interrupt latency is largely determined by the interrupt controller circuit and its configuration. They can also affect the jitter in the interrupt latency, which can drastically affect the real-time schedulability of the system. The Intel APIC Architecture is well known for producing a huge amount of interrupt latency jitter.

Maximum interrupt latency is largely determined by the methods an OS uses for interrupt handling. For example, most processors allow programs to disable interrupts, putting off the execution of interrupt handlers, in order to protect critical sections of code. During the execution of such a critical section, all interrupt handlers that cannot execute safely within a critical section are blocked (they save the minimum amount of information required to restart the interrupt handler after all critical sections have exited). So, the interrupt latency for a blocked interrupt is extended to the end of the critical section, plus any interrupts with equal and higher priority that arrived while the block was in place.

Many computer systems require low interrupt latencies, especially embedded systems that need to control machinery in real-time. Sometimes, these systems use a real-time operating system (RTOS). A RTOS makes the promise that no more than an agreed upon maximum amount of time will pass between executions of subroutines. In order to do this, the RTOS must also guarantee that interrupt latency will never exceed a predefined maximum.

There are many methods that hardware may use to increase the interrupt latency that can be tolerated. These include buffers, and flow control.

For example, most network cards implement transmit and receive ring buffers, interrupt rate limiting, and hardware flow control. Buffers allow data to be stored until it can be transferred, and flow control allows the network card to pause communications without having to discard data if the buffer is full.

Modern hardware also implements interrupt rate limiting. This helps prevent **interrupt storms or *live lock*** by having the hardware wait a programmable minimum amount of time between each interrupt it generators. Interrupt rate limiting reduces the amount of time spent servicing interrupts, allowing the processor to spend more time doing useful work. Exceeding this time results in a soft (recoverable) or hard (non-recoverable) error.

If the function *f*( ) does not complete even after t_1 time units have elapsed, then the watchdog timer expires, indicating that the task deadline is missed and the exception handling procedure is initiated.

In case the task completes before the watchdog timer expires (*i.e.,* the task completes within its deadline), then the watchdog timer is reset using a **wd-Tickle( )** Call.

I/O SYSTEMS

I/O sub-systems are an important part of **OS** services.

Example : The **UART** access and the **similar port** access.

I/O parts are the subsystems of OS device management systems. Drivers to communicate with the many devices of them. I/O instruction depend on the **Hardware platform.**

I/O systems differ in the different OSs.

I/O Subsystem in a Typical I/O System in an OS

Subsystem Hierarchy	*Actions and layers between the subsystems*
Application	An Application having an I/O system. There may be a sub-layer between the application and I/O basic functions buffered I/O or I/O library functions for **read and write** functions.
I/O Basic functions	These are device independent OS functions. There may be a sub-layer between application and I/O basic functions and I/O device driver functions File System functions for **read and write** functions.
I/O device driver functions	These are device dependent OS functions. Device drive functions a driver may interface with a set of library functions. Example: Serial communicate.
Device Hardware (or) Port (or) I/O interface card	Serial Device (or) Network.

WATCHDOG TIMER/TIMERS

RTOS normally support two main types of timers

- Periodic timers
- Aperiodic timers **(one shot)** timers.

Periodic Timers

Periodic timers are used mainly for sampling events at regular intervals( ) performing some activity's periodically. Once a periodic timer is set, it expires periodically.

Aperiodic timer

These timers are set to expire only once.

Watchdog timers are a popular example of one shot timers.

Aperiodic timers sometimes also called as **"one shot timers".**

Watchdog timers are used extensively in **R.T programs** to detect **if a task misses its deadline** and then to initiate exception handling procedure upon a deadline miss.

An Example : Use of a watchdog timer has been shown illustrated.

In **Figure** a watchdog timer is set at the start of a certain **critical function** *f* ( ) through a **wd_start (t_1)** call. The **wd_start (t_2)** call sets the watchdog timer to expire by the specified deadline (t_1 time units) from the starting of the task.

```
f( )

{    ^
     |
     |   wd_start_(t1, Exception-Handler);        <---- start
     |
     |        :
t1   v        :
              :

         wd_Tickle ( );                           <---- END
}
```

❑❑❑

INDEX

L

M

O

P

R

S

T

V

W

❑❑❑

❑❑❑